PROUD TO SERVE

MEMOIRS

Edward A. Trautt
Colonel US Air Force (Ret.)

Copies available from:
www.createspace.com/3775308
www.amazon.com

DEDICATION

DIVINE PROVIDENCE smiled kindly and generously upon me as I journeyed down life's highway. In grateful appreciation, I dedicate this collection of my memoirs to my gracious wife, our ten wonderful children and my parents.

My wife Ludmila (Perebaskine) Trautt, nick - named "Toussia," is a generous, caring and humble, "Grand Lady." She is my priceless jewel, a most wonderful and understanding wife. Indeed, she makes friends easily and is well liked by all who know her.

Davis, CA, 1995

Our 10 children in 1995, at my 80th birthday party, Davis, CA

Each of our ten children, though so much alike in good character, has his or her own specific and special personality traits and talents. After observing their growing-up years and knowing them now as mature adults, I recognize one common denominator that characterizes or personalizes all of them. That common denominator is compassion. It pleases me greatly to know that, as adults, they all are our friends. They all are especially wonderful, generous, and loving children, each of whom we love dearly. I hope and pray that they will find much happiness and great success in all their endeavors, as they journey down life's highway.

I also dedicate this book to the memory of both my parents, John James Trautt and Margaret Anna (Arbes) Trautt. Their wisdom, spirituality and compassion had a significant influence upon my life.

John and Margaret Trautt,
summer of 1953

ACKNOWLEDGMENTS

I WISH TO ACKNOWLEDGE the many persons who provided encouragement, assistance, and/or contributed in other ways to bring this book to fruition. I thank my wife Ludmila, for her help, support and encouragement, my daughter Irene, for her patience, diligence and many long hours putting my words to print, and my daughters Mary and Elizabeth for carefully reviewing several drafts and providing gentle recommendations and edits.

CONTENTS

PART ONE

HUMBLE BEGINNINGS

FARMING FAMILY

I WAS BORN A FARMBOY in Akron, Iowa on April 29, 1915, fifth born of eleven children. My siblings and I are second generation Americans on our two grandmothers' sides, and our grandfathers were both immigrants. My dad's father, James Edward Trautt, emigrated alone from Ireland to the United States in 1863, at the tender age of 15, looking for employment. My mom's father, Wenzel Arbes, emigrated with his family from Bohemia when he was four years old, in 1869. Both of my mother's parents spoke German at home, and she did not learn English until she started school. Our family tree is included at the end of this chapter.

My father who was born and raised on a farm, the oldest of eight children, was able to attend school only between harvest time and spring planting. When he was in eighth grade, he assumed primary responsibility for management of the family farm. Although he had a limited formal education, dad acquired considerable agricultural skills and knowledge of animal husbandry managing the farm, and he was widely read, and self-educated.

Unfortunately, while my dad was growing up, his father, my grandpa, had too much interest in drinking with his friends and dreaming up schemes to get rich quick, than managing the farm. Grandpa died a gruesome death when my dad was 27. It was on a Saturday night, July 6, 1907, when grandpa, James Edward Trautt, then 59 years old, was walking home after a long day of celebrating with his friends. His fatal mistake was choosing to take a short cut home by way of the railroad tracks, and being caught in a narrow cut with no escape from a fast moving freight train, when it came upon him. The story of his accident, full of graphic details, appeared in all the local papers.

My dad continued to manage his parent's farm for two more years after grandpa died, until at age 29, he married my mother. He remained a tenant farmer for most of my childhood. Before she married my father, my mother was a school teacher in a one-room country schoolhouse.

My parents, John and Margaret (Arbes) Trautt,
on their wedding day in 1909.

During my childhood, we moved several times due to unfortunate and unforeseen circumstances. We lived in northwestern Iowa, until we relocated out of state to Herbster, Wisconsin where I started 11th grade.

Pictured above are my parents and their first 5 children, on our farm in Akron, Iowa, *circa 1915*. I am in my mom's arms and in the foreground are my four older brothers, left to right, Lyle, Norbert, Vincent, and Robert.

I remember my parents as being spiritually humble and compassionate. They truly lived a life of faith, hope and charity.

On our family farms, we usually had about eight workhorses, seven or eight milk cows, sometimes a goat or a mule, some geese, several domestic grey rabbits, a flock of Muscovy flying ducks, some turkeys, always a large number of chickens, a large flock of pigeons and, of course, dogs and cats. Our main cash crops produced were corn, wheat, oats and alfalfa/clover hay. We also had a very large vegetable garden where we grew mostly potatoes, cabbage, tomatoes, carrots, melons and onions for sale in the marketplace. In the remainder of the garden, we grew all kinds of vegetables for home use like cucumbers, radishes, green onions, rhubarb, leaf lettuce and herbs like dill, etc.

Like most small family farms in those days, we sometimes employed a live-in farmhand. This was still the era of horse-drawn farm equipment, tractors came a few years later. It still amazes me just how much foodstuff my dad, one farmhand and a bunch of horses could produce in those days, when everything was just plain hard manual labor without benefit of power machines and equipment. I am further amazed at just how self-sufficient the family farm was.

My dad built his own tool and machine shop. He installed industrial machines and equipment, including grinding wheels, wood and metal turning lathes, circular saws and a large forge and anvil. All the equipment was operated from a long metal drive shaft with pulleys and belts to each machine. Each machine could be operated independently or all could be used simultaneously.

Dad built his own smoke house and each autumn he slaughtered beef and pork for processing into sausage, bacon, ham and dried beef in the smoke house. We had a machine to grind wheat, corn and oats into home use flours. Almost every Saturday, my mother baked whole grain loaves of bread using her own live cultured yeast which she perpetuated in the kitchen on a shelf above the wood-burning kitchen stove

As a youngster, I remember my dad always experimenting with and seeking to genetically improve grains, especially corn. During harvest season, he would select ears of corn for whatever special quality he desired, such as size of ear and early harvest. I recall one experiment that he worked on for three or four years which resulted in the development of a small ear of yellow corn that ripened earlier than the other corn. In fact, the corn took about ninety days from planting to harvest and became known locally as the ninety day wonder corn. At the time, the available varieties of corn matured in about 100-110 days.

During the harvest season, mom canned all kinds of fruits and vegetables and made crocks of sauerkraut and dill pickles and other preserved foods.

Each spring, after school was out, mom would make soap, always more than enough to last until next year's event. Making home-made soap is actually quite simple, though a messy and day-long process. To make soap, the previous winter's ashes from wood burning stoves were added to autumn's rendered animal fats (tallow) and boiled in a 30 or 40 gallon cast iron kettle over an open wood fire. The boiling mixture was stirred with a wooden paddle until soap and glycerin were formed.

When mom made soap she would periodically check the boiling mixture watching for the soap to separate out on top of a liquid solution of glycerin. Somehow, she could always tell when it had cooked long enough. To stop the boil after the soap and glycerin were separated, the fire would no longer be fueled. After it had cooled a bit, the glycerin was drained through a faucet on the bottom of the kettle.

The still warm soap would be skimmed out of the kettle and placed in tubs to cool and harden. A few days later, the soap was cut into small bars, ready for use. The residue of soapy ashes was also dried and cut into small bars to be used for scouring and cleaning cookware. The glycerin by-product would be sold to a chemical company in Sioux City.

When the Great Depression started, I was twelve years old. Like so many other families during those tough ensuing years, ours struggled to make ends meet and put food on the table. Fortunately, industriousness, resourcefulness and ingenuity was a way of life in our farming tradition, we fared better than many. My mother was a cook, baker, seamstress, gardener, nurse, teacher, musician, artist, soap-maker and a full-time wife and mother of ten children. And, my dad, he could build and/or repair any machine or tool or structure he needed on the farm with the machine shop he designed and constructed.

As children, we helped where we could, earning money

and shouldering responsibilities for tending crops and farm animals. When farming and bartering wasn't enough during the depression, dad's considerable carpentry, mechanical and management skills helped him find odd jobs and eventually landed him coveted city jobs when they were available. But, even in the city, we never left our farming roots behind, and always planted large gardens in our backyard, or vacant city lots.

GENEALOGY

Edward's and Ludmila's Ancestors

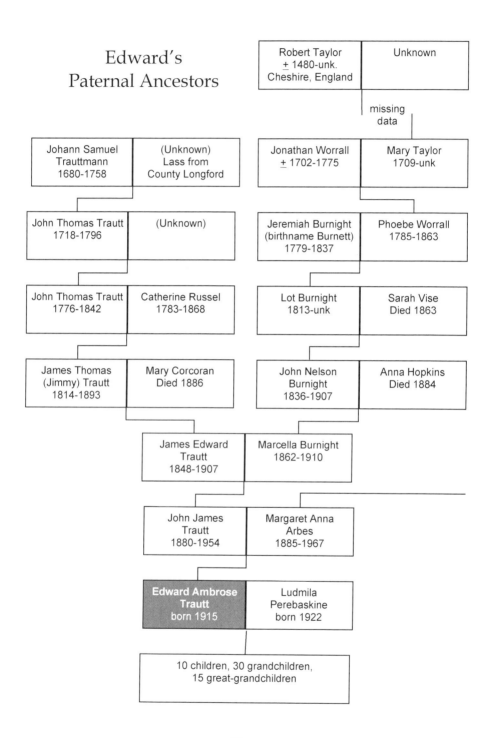

Edward's
Paternal Ancestors

Robert Taylor + 1480-unk. Cheshire, England	Unknown

missing data

Johann Samuel Trauttmann 1680-1758	(Unknown) Lass from County Longford

Jonathan Worrall + 1702-1775	Mary Taylor 1709-unk

John Thomas Trautt 1718-1796	(Unknown)

Jeremiah Burnight (birthname Burnett) 1779-1837	Phoebe Worrall 1785-1863

John Thomas Trautt 1776-1842	Catherine Russel 1783-1868

Lot Burnight 1813-unk	Sarah Vise Died 1863

James Thomas (Jimmy) Trautt 1814-1893	Mary Corcoran Died 1886

John Nelson Burnight 1836-1907	Anna Hopkins Died 1884

James Edward Trautt 1848-1907	Marcella Burnight 1862-1910

John James Trautt 1880-1954	Margaret Anna Arbes 1885-1967

Edward Ambrose Trautt born 1915	Ludmila Perebaskine born 1922

10 children, 30 grandchildren, 15 great-grandchildren

Edward's
Maternal Ancestors

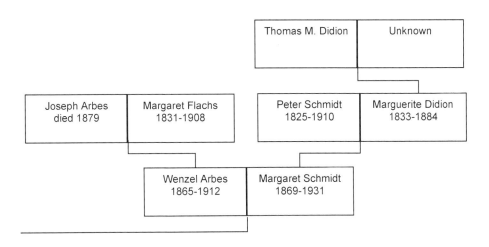

Additional Ancestral Information for Edward A. Trautt

Name	Birth	Death	Spouse
Arbes, Joseph	Bohemia	10-15-1879, USA Springfield, Minnesota	Flachs, Margaret
Arbes, Margaret Anna	10-29-1885, USA Windom, MN	2-11-1967, USA Alton, IL	Trautt, John James
Arbes, Wenzel	1865, Bohemia	1912, USA Windom, Minnesota	Schmidt, Margaret
Burnight, Jeremiah	12-12-1813, Scotland birth name "Burnett"	11-8-1837 USA Marion, Indiana	Worrall, Phoebe
Burnight, John Nelson	6-29-1836, USA Lebanon, Pennsylvania	12-25-1907, USA Akron, Iowa	Hopkins, Anna
Burnight, Lot	12-12-1813, USA Lebanon, Pennsylvania	USA Orland, California	Vise, Sara
Burnight, Marcella	10-22-1862, USA Akron, IA	3-23-1910, USA Akron, IA	Trautt, James Edward
Corcoran, Mary	Ireland County Longford	11-1886, Ireland County Longford	Trautt, James (Jimmy) Thomas
Didion, Marguerite (aka Mrs. Margaret Schach)	12-15-1833, France	4-25-1884, USA Windom, Minnesota	Schmidt, Peter
Didion, Thomas M.	19th Century, France	19th Century, USA	Unknown
Flachs, Margaret	9-18-1831, Bohemia	11-2-1908, USA Jeffers, Minnesota	Arbes, Joseph
Hopkins, Anna	Ireland, County Longford	12-17-1884, USA Akron, Iowa	Burnight, John Nelson
Perebaskine, Ludmila	2-24-1922, Yugoslavia Zemoun	n/a	Trautt, Edward Ambrose
Russel, Catherine	Unknown, likely England	Unknown	Trautt, John Thomas II
Schmidt, Margaret	5-28-1869, USA St. Peter, Minnesota	1931, USA Sioux City, Iowa	Arbes, Wenzel
Schmidt, Peter	11-28-1825, Germany	3-2-1910, USA Windom, Minnesota	Didion, Marguerite
Taylor, Mary	4-21-1709, USA Pennsylvania	USA Pennsylvania	Worrall, Jonathan
Taylor, Robert	± 1480, England Cheshire	Unknown	Wife Unknown
Trautt, Edward Ambrose	4-29-1915, USA Akron, Iowa	n/a	Perebaskine, Ludmila

Trautt, James (Jimmy) Thomas	12-1814, Ireland Ardagh	4-21-1893, Ireland Ardagh	Corcoran, Mary
Trautt, James Edward	3-16-1848, Ireland Ardagh	7-6-1907, USA Mt. Vernon, Ohio	Burnight, Marcella
Trautt, John James	2-1-1880, USA Monticello, Iowa	9-12-1954, Wood River, Illinois	Arbes, Margaret Anna
Trautt, John Thomas	1718, Ireland Ardagh	1796, Ireland Ardagh	Unknown wife, married in 1768
Trautt, John Thomas II	1776, Ireland Ardagh	1842, Ireland Ardagh	Russel, Catherine
Trauttmann, Johann Samuel	1680, Germany Rhineland	1758, Ireland County Longford	Unknown wife, married + 1711 from Lisnaugh, Ireland
Vise, Sara	USA Indiana	1863, USA Jones, Iowa	Burnight, Lot
Worrall, Jonathan	+ 1702, USA Delaware, Pennsylvania	+ 1775, USA	Taylor, Mary
Worrall, Phoebe	4-9-1785, USA Delaware, PN	12-21-1863, USA Jones, IA	Burnight, Jeremiah

Ludmila's Ancestors

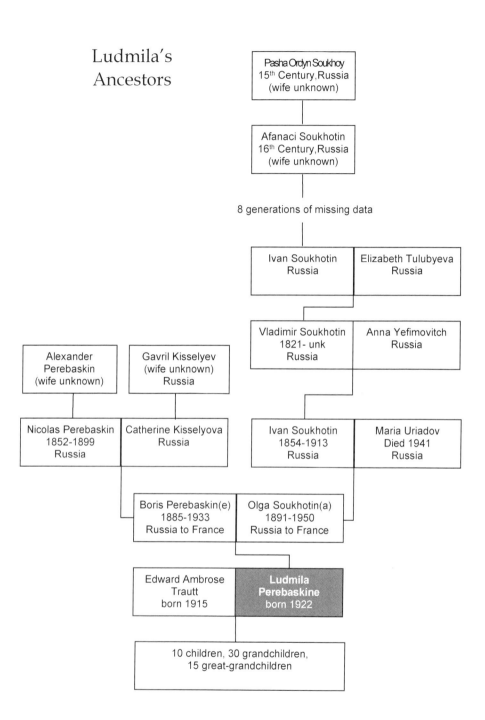

Pasha Ordyn Soukhoy
15th Century, Russia
(wife unknown)

Afanaci Soukhotin
16th Century, Russia
(wife unknown)

8 generations of missing data

Ivan Soukhotin
Russia

Elizabeth Tulubyeva
Russia

Vladimir Soukhotin
1821- unk
Russia

Anna Yefimovitch
Russia

Alexander
Perebaskin
(wife unknown)

Gavril Kisselyev
(wife unknown)
Russia

Nicolas Perebaskin
1852-1899
Russia

Catherine Kisselyova
Russia

Ivan Soukhotin
1854-1913
Russia

Maria Uriadov
Died 1941
Russia

Boris Perebaskin(e)
1885-1933
Russia to France

Olga Soukhotin(a)
1891-1950
Russia to France

Edward Ambrose
Trautt
born 1915

Ludmila
Perebaskine
born 1922

10 children, 30 grandchildren,
15 great-grandchildren

Additional Perebaskin(e) Ancestral Information

Name	Birth	Death	Spouse
Kisselyev, Gavril	Russia	Russia	Wife unknown
Kisselyova, Catherine	Russia	Russia	Perebaskin, Nicolas
Perebaskin(e), Boris	6-8-1885, Russia St. Petersburg	3-1-1933, France Strasburg	Soukhotin(a), Olga
Perebaskin, Alexander	Russia	Russia	Wife unknown
Perebaskin, Nicolas	1852, Russia St. Petersburg,	1899, Russia	Kissselyova, Catherine
Perebaskine, Ludmila	2-4-1922, Serbia/Yugoslavia Zemoun	n/a	Trautt, Edward Ambrose
Soukhotin(a), Olga	2-17-1891,Russia Vladivostok, Siberia	5-4-1950, France Paris	Perebaskin(e), Boris
Soukhotin, Afanaci	16th Century, Russia	Same	Wife unknown
Soukhotin, Ivan	Russia	Russia	Tulbyeva, Elizabeth
Soukhotin, Ivan	2-24-1854, Russia St. Petersburg	1913, Russia	Uriadov, Maria
Soukhotin, Vladimir	1821, Russia	Russia	Yefimovitch, Anna
Soukhov, Pasha Ordyn	15th Century, Russia	Same	Wife unknown
Trautt, Edward Ambrose	4-29-1915, USA Akron, Iowa	n/a	Perebaskine, Ludmila
Tulubyeva, Elizabeth	Russia	Russia	Soukhotin, Ivan
Uriadov, Maria	Russia Vladivostok, Siberia	1941, Russia	Soukhotin, Ivan
Yefimovitch, Anna	Russia	Russia	Soukhotin, Vladimir

EARLY CHILDHOOD

I HAD MY FIRST ENCOUNTER with strawberries when I was about two years old. I remember the story from my mom reciting it to me over the years. That spring on the farm, as always, we had a very large vegetable garden which included a large patch of strawberries. When it came time to pick the first ripe strawberries of the season, my mother assembled my older brothers to pick the strawberries. Mom picked me up and took me along and sat me down at the edge of the berry patch.

Strawberry picking commenced and as each person completed picking a row, they would drop off the berries into a bowl placed close to me. Soon, mom announced it was time to go back to the house and prepare the season's first yield of strawberries for dessert. The season's first picking never produces much yield and the ripe berries are typically small, but delicious. What a surprise they had when they came to collect what was supposed to be strawberry topping for short cake! Surprise doesn't quite describe the event. There I sat, an empty bowl next to me, my face and shirt smeared red with strawberry juice and not one strawberry in sight.

My mother, in shock, finally got her composure and managed to ask, "Oh my God, did you eat all the berries?"

As mom told it so many times years later, I calmly looked up and blurted out, "I wike skrawburries!"

While growing up on the family farm, hardly a day passed without something funny, enjoyable or exciting happening. During harvest season, dad was kept extremely busy hauling wagon loads of produce to Sioux City markets and stores a few miles away. One or two of us kids would always get to go along on the six to eight hour, daytime trips. The day came when it was my turn and my younger brother Cyril's turn. We were ready and eager to go. We took our places on a big wooden seat at the top and front of the horse-drawn wagon, and off we went to Sioux City. The wagon was filled to the brim with potatoes, carrots, tomatoes and onions.

After selling the produce, we headed for the bakery where broken cookies and crackers were separated into one-bushel baskets for sale cheap. Would you believe it?! On every trip, dad would buy one basket of each (cookies and soda crackers) and then go to the grocery store to buy lunch meats, cheese, sardines, soft drinks and whatever was on sale and good to eat. On that particular trip, some wooden buckets filled with 25 pounds of hard candies were on sale for almost nothing. He bought one bucket. It seems to me that he paid about $1.00 for the candy and about two dollars for each bushel box of broken cookies and crackers.

About midday it was time to enjoy the fruits (so to speak) of our victorious trek to the big city. This was the part of the trip that we all enjoyed the most, not that we didn't enjoy everything about the trip to such an awful big city. There was a public park, with benches, drinking water faucets, toilets, bar-be-cue pits, picnic tables--the works--directly on our way home. That was truly the most exciting part of the day, eating grocery cold cuts and cheese sandwiches, broken crackers, soda pop, with all kinds of broken cookies and mixed hard candy for dessert. You'll never get closer to "Hawg Heaven" than that--and we truly did pig out.

Not wanting to miss a thing during this trip, my first time ever in a big city, I was all eyes. I noticed some kids playing in a vacant lot near the road. I couldn't believe how dark their skin was and asked my dad, "How could those kids get so dirty? They must have been playing in a coal pile all day. I'll bet they'll catch it from their mom when they get home!" That was the first time in my life that I had ever seen a person of color. I remember my dad told me that it wasn't coal dust on them, that they were just boys like me but with darker skin. We were relatively isolated in the small farming communities where I grew up. Most of the prejudice we witnessed was religious intolerance, not racial. My parents set an example for us kids by treating others, especially neighbors, as they hoped others would treat them.

.

DEVASTATING EPIDEMIC

WHEN I WAS ALMOST FOUR YEARS OLD, in the winter of I918-19, a flu epidemic spread across America. It was sometimes called the Spanish or German Flu, now known as the 1918 Flu, or the WW I Influenza Virus. It devastated some communities, with many households in our community suffering at least one or more deaths. As best I can recollect from my own memory and also from what my mother explained to me some years later, I'll relate the story of how the flu epidemic affected our family.

My older brother Vincent, my younger brother Cyril and I became seriously ill. In those days it was common for doctors to make house calls by horse and buggy. As our illness worsened, the doctor visited us daily. One day after our temperatures soared to critical heights, the doctor told my folks that, if the fevers didn't subside, he didn't expect the three of us to survive the night.

Early the following morning, Cyril's and my fevers slowly started to drop. Mom phoned the lower temperature readings to the doctor. He told her that was the sign he was waiting for and that Cyril and I were probably out of serious danger. Although our fevers had subsided, Vincent's had not. All through that previous night and the next morning Vincent's fever continued to rise slowly and steadily. Near noon on January 19, 1918, Vincent's frail, exhausted, feverish little body expired. Some years later, my mother told me that when Vincent was about two or three he had been afflicted with what the doctor later believed to have been infantile (polio) paralysis. The disease left him paralyzed from the waist down. I still remember how, before he became ill with the flu, he would crawl around the house and pull himself up to the windows to look outside. He was probably left weak and frail after the bout with polio and not strong enough to overcome the flu.

Although no one told me that Vincent had died, I sensed it. I had seen two men in white jackets wheel his body, on a hospital gurney, down the hall past my room and toward the front door. A little later, mom came to my room. I asked, "Where are they taking Vincent?" She bent over close to me and quietly said, "Vincent is going to heaven."

Cyril's and my condition steadily improved. In a couple of days Cyril was out of bed and doing very well, with no residual effects. It took me longer to recover. And, when I was finally well enough to get out of bed, I had developed complications from the flu, and found it painful and difficult to bend my arms and legs at the elbows and knees. The doctor prescribed hot baths, daily massages and manual movement of the elbow and knee joints. In a few weeks, my elbows were almost back to normal but my knees were still quite stiff and I waddled like a duck. The doctor was worried that I might never walk normally again. After a few more months of therapy, the doctor was amazed at my progress. The prescribed therapy was to walk-walk-walk. So, I walked 'n walked 'n walked 'n walked.

A year later, my gait was much better, and my parents continued to encourage me to walk about, to improve my strength and gait. I loved living on the farm, it seemed like the whole world to me, and I guess it was. We had everything imaginable, a black walnut grove, large expansive fields of grain, fields of clover and alfalfa, pasture land with a creek and all kinds of animals (including three different sizes of ponies to ride), a wind mill water pump, a creek to swim in naked, a nice outhouse featuring a seat made from a nice wood board, and complete with our own Sears and Roebuck catalog.

I still remember the old hard coal heater centered at the end of our large living room. The combined heat from that heater and the wood-fueled, cast iron cook stove was enough to warm the entire two-story house. Often, on cold winter nights, Mr. Tom Brady, our hired farmhand, would sit by the coal heater in a huge oak rocking chair and tell tall tales about his escapades of hunting big game and whopper fish stories, as all of us kids sat around listening in awe. After a few winters listening to Mr. Brady's stories, those big ferocious "black barrs" (bears) and hordes of vicious wild lions and tigers were increasingly interesting and almost real.

I realize now, that it was only a matter of time until our little imaginations would take the reigns. Visualize the setting, a warm but drizzly summer day, two little boys, a four year old and a five year old, playing in the rain--each boy with a big stick for a gun to pretend hunting "big, black, ferocious barrs", just like those in Mr. Brady's stories, and, not only is it raining, but there is a pretty good sized creek, about one-quarter mile from the house, which is steadily rising from the rain.

We two boys, my little brother Cyril and I, had been barr huntin' for some time in our front yard, and we got caught up in our barr huntin' adventure. Soon we were headed out of the yard's safe environment in search of dangerous barrs in the wooded area on the nearby creek banks. The creek banks in reality, were far more dangerous to us than those imaginary bears.

Shortly before supper, someone in the family realized that two of the clan were missing. Someone was sent out in the drizzle to check the barn, machine shop and storage sheds. When it was reported back to mom and dad that they were nowhere to be found, all pandemonium broke out. Dad took charge and called the farmhand to help form a search party. The hired hand was sent to the walnut grove and the older brothers were told to stay in the house and wait, just in case two lost little boys showed up. Mom and dad headed toward the creek, about a five or ten minute walk from the house. Dad went upstream and mom went downstream.

After a short distance, mom noticed some barely visible little footprints in the mud on the edge of the rising water of the creek. As mom told the story years later, when she saw those footprints but no sign of the two little bear hunters, she let out a blood-curdling scream and dad came running. Together, they followed the footprints for only a few more yards when mom spotted Turk, our family dog, on the creek bank about twenty yards away. Old Turk, a big all-white collie, appeared almost frantic going up and down the bank and walking almost in a circle.

Mom and dad both ran as fast as possible. Dad arrived first with mom close behind. They found both of us immobilized in the mud, only about three or four feet above the rising water.

Dad said sternly, "What are you kids doing out here?"

There I was, stuck in the mud, one shoe missing, cold, hungry and totally exhausted.

I meekly replied, "We're huntin' a big black barr."

Dad pulled me out of the mud after a strong jerk and then even more sternly said, "Now, you walk!"

Cyril was exhausted and almost asleep as mom pulled him out of the mud and handed him to dad who carried him home. Mom held my hand as we walked all the way home, me with one foot in a shoe full of mud, the other foot bare.

It was probably less than a quarter mile back to the house, but, tired and cold as I was, it seemed like ten. We both were given a warm bath, a bowl of hot chicken soup and tucked into bed. Mom told us years later that we slept all night and until about noon the next day. That was the first, the last and the only time we went "barr huntin."

PART 2

GROWING UP

PRIMARY EDUCATION

IN MY CHILDHOOD, there was no kindergarten and the rule was that children were not allowed to start first grade until they reached the age of six on or before their first day of school. So, the summer after turning six years old in April, 1921, my mother enrolled me at St. Patrick Catholic School in Akron, Iowa and I started first grade in September that same year.

For some time, almost every day when I came home from school, mom would ask, "How was your day and what did you have for dinner?" In those days, that's what we called our mid-day meal. I would list the foods we had and she would reply, "Oh boy, I sure would like some of that!"

One day we were served wieners (hot dogs). I took a bite, then remembered how mom always said she would sure like some of our food. I looked around to make sure no one noticed, then quickly put the hot dog in my pocket.

When the meal supervisor came by checking everyone's plates, she commented, "My, you were hungry, too. You ate everything."

Just imagine what that hot dog must have looked like by five o'clock, after carrying it in my pocket all afternoon on that warm Indian summer day. When I arrived home, I excitedly ran up to mom and exclaimed, "Look what I brought for you from school!"

Can you imagine the surprised expression on her face, when I handed her that cold, shriveled, dried up, partly eaten hotdog. Now that I think about it, I think I know what crossed her mind as she took that hot dog and politely said, "Oh, thank you for remembering me." She did gently suggest, however, that I probably should not bring any more food home. Years later, when I was in college, she told me that our dog Turk really enjoyed eating that wiener.

That first school year started out fine and I was really enjoying my new friends and school. But, shortly into the year I became very sick with an undiagnosed illness, followed by measles and then chicken pox. I missed so much school that academic year due to illness, that I was required to repeat first grade.

Fortunately, during the summer break, I stayed well and had time to recuperate. I played outside all summer and did a lot of walking. At a follow-up medical examination in late August, everything looked fine, and although my knees were still slightly stiff from the influenza virus I had survived three years before, I was able to run slowly and play with the other kids.

So, in September, 1922, I was enrolled again in first grade at St. Patrick School. More than seven years old at the time, I was ready and anxious to make up for lost time. That was a very good year for me, I really enjoyed school and all my friends at school. Even more important, I was seldom sick that entire school year.

Whenever my children complained about how they got to school, I jokingly told them that I had to walk five miles to school, in deep snow, in sub-zero weather, uphill both ways. As they grew older they realized the truth and added, "yes, and barefoot, too!"

When I was in first grade at St. Patrick's, we would arise at about 6:30 A.M. each school day, dress, eat breakfast, layout our coats and be ready for a buggy ride to school about three miles from our farm house. School started at 9:00 A.M. and ended at 4:00 P.M.

Lyle, my oldest brother, was responsible for harnessing the horse and hitching it up to the one-horse buggy. He would put a bail of hay, a horse's drinking bucket and grain in the buggy for the horse. In the winter time we each heated a clay brick in the oven of our big wood-burning kitchen cook stove and wrapped it in newspaper and a cloth bag to keep our feet warm. We had a big black bear skin blanket to keep our bodies warm on the trip to school.

One very cool and frosty school day morning in late autumn, Lyle about scared the wits out of the whole family. He was harnessing the horse, as he did every school day, but this particular day he was careless, which resulted in the horse kicking him in the face. I had just gone outside to put something for school in the buggy, when I saw Lyle as he burst screaming through the barn door, his face covered with blood. I ran back into the house, yelling for mom and dad. Mom rushed Lyle into the house and wrapped his head in towels, while dad hurriedly finished harnessing the horse and hitching it to the buggy. They put Lyle in the buggy on mom's lap and took off for the hospital in Akron, about 3 miles away, as fast as that horse could run.

Lyle's nose was kicked off his face, hanging only by the skin on one side. The operation to remove bone fragments, sew his nose back on his head and bandage him up took almost four hours. To say the least, he missed quite a few days of school. Norbert, our second oldest brother, became the new buggy driver. After several days of healing, Lyle was breathing normally again through his nose. However, the tear duct of his left eye was permanently damaged and from then on he suffered with dry eye irritation during windy or low humidity weather conditions.

After my second year in first grade at St. Patrick's, the Westfield school board expanded its district boundaries to include our area of the township. The Westfield Public School was about a mile closer to our farm house than St. Patrick's Catholic School in Akron. The really good news was that a horse drawn school wagon provided transport for the students in the area to and from school.

By August that summer of 1923, my brothers and I were

enrolled in the Westfield Public School, me in second grade. No more preparing our horse and buggy for the ride to school, just dress, eat breakfast, prepare a dinner (lunch) bucket and wait for the school bus (wagon) to arrive.

After about a couple of months of school, one of the neighbor boys was beginning to be routinely late for the wagon/bus. The driver warned his mother about it and told her that he would no longer hold up the bus for her child. After a few days, the boy was again late. The driver did as he said and drove on without waiting for him. Then, a few days later, another morning, the bus driver came to the boy's empty bus stop and was about to drive on, when suddenly, his mother came running out of the house carrying the boy, his shoes and clothes. She opened the bus door, threw in the shoes and clothes and shoved the boy in. She declared, "Now, maybe you will get dressed!" And then, she slammed the door shut and the driver drove on.

There stood the fifth grade boy, stark naked, frozen like a statue, in shock and totally embarrassed. About half of the students were girls. With much fumbling and some help from one of the older girls who was handing him his clothes, he finally got dressed. He was never late again, but I don't know if he ever got over the shame of his severe lesson in tardiness.

UNHAPPILY A NEW HOME

I ENJOYED SECOND GRADE in the Westfield school and had missed but a few school days and those were due to only minor illness. I made many friends, both boys and girls. We all passed into the next grade and I was looking forward to our usual busy summer on the farm. That July, 1924, with the summer vacation well underway, we were informed that we would have to move out at the end of summer. This couldn't have happened at a worse time for us. The economy throughout the nation was in a terrible slump and financial conditions were bad everywhere.

We had lived on that 160-acre farm since 1909, it was owned by my fathers' uncle, Thomas Lot Burnight. My parents were newlyweds when they moved into that home with my oldest brother Lyle and my maternal grandmother. Eight more children were born to them in that home, including me. Only my youngest two brothers were born after we moved on.

Uncle Burnight had always been very fond of my dad and was happy to make his property available to him to farm. They even had a verbal agreement that someday, my father would purchase the property. But, that was not to be. Uncle Burnight died unexpectedly, on June 22, 1917, at the age of 58 following surgery for appendicitis. The LeMars Sentinel newspaper published an obituary , on July 31, 1917, describing Thomas as a well known pioneer who rose from poverty to affluence, calling him "one of Akron's most generally esteemed and influential citizens and businessmen."

After Uncle Thomas died, his widow and his son, my

father's cousin, Thomas Louis Burnight, inherited the property. Cousin Thomas allowed our family to continue renting the property, and entered into a lease for another seven years after his father died, until August of 1924. Before the end of the lease, Cousin Thomas covertly sold the property to a Mr. Greene, and that new owner expected us to vacate the property at the end of the lease.

My parents had been unaware of the sale until just a few months before the lease ended. Apparently, Cousin Thomas sold the property out from under us because some of dad's brothers tried to take Cousin Thomas' inheritance, claiming he was not the biological son of Uncle Thomas. Cousin Thomas was furious and erroneously believed my dad was a party to the feud. The bad blood turned young Thomas against our relatives and my dad, too. Much later, Cousin Thomas learned the truth that dad was not involved in the claim, and had actually opposed it. He came to dad, apologetic about selling the farm, but, it was too late, the property had been sold and we had moved away from our long-time home.

As soon as we found out we needed to vacate the property, my dad immediately started looking for another farm to rent. Within weeks of our deadline to leave, dad had found nothing available, except a rundown 80-acre farm in the less fertile hill country near Merrill, Iowa, only a few miles away.

Due to the short notice to vacate by September, in desperation, dad moved our family temporarily into a rental house in Akron, Iowa, about 3 miles away. Meanwhile, he continued looking for a suitable farm to rent. Unable to find anything else, he made arrangements to rent the Merrill hill country farm. That farm had a fairly good house, several storage sheds and a large, new storage barn for animals and hay. It was quite a change from the larger and fully equipped Burnight farm.

What to do?! We had too much of everything for a small 80-acre farm. There was nothing else dad could do but sell that year's crops and the surplus livestock and machinery.

With the economy in shambles nearing the Great Depression, our public auction sale in August, 1924 was a dismal failure. The local farmers had little or no money and couldn't get loans to purchase our animals or farm machinery. When the animals and equipment did finally sell, they went for about one-fourth their actual value.

The next fiasco was moving the remaining animals and equipment to the new farm. Finally, by late October, dad had moved all our property from what was now the Greene's farm, onto the new hill country farm. Everything on that 80 acre farm would be on a smaller scale than what we were accustomed to. We no longer required the hired hand. He was immediately missed, especially by us kids who had so enjoyed his hunting and fishing stories. He soon found another farmhand job in the area, to that family's good fortune.

By early November, 1924, we were settled into the house in the hill country. All of us children were enrolled in a country school named Sleepy Hollow. I was entering third grade and anxious to go to school and meet all those new kids. Our new farm was about one mile or so from school, so we walked to school.

Sleepy Hollow school was a one room building with one teacher for grades one through eight. About 30 or more students attended that school. It wasn't anything like the two schools which we had previously attended in Akron and Westfield. Picture this, desks that consisted of wood tables and benches, a pot-bellied, flattop wood-burning stove for heat, an outside water well, an outhouse with a Sears catalog and a pasture behind the school to tie up the students' horses. In winter, the teacher and students kept soup on the stove top to eat with our noon meal.

There was no indoor plumbing at the school or in most of the homes during that era. Water at the school was hand pumped from a shallow outside well. Occasionally, the winter nighttime temperature would drop well below freezing and the pump would freeze up. By mid-afternoon the pump would usually thaw enough to water the horses. The teacher always kept a reserve tank of drinking water inside of the school for the students.

In those days, most rural homes and one-room schoolhouses did not have indoor toilets. Instead, they were equipped with a small one-door outhouse (privy), placed over a dug out hole in the ground. The outhouse toilet seat was simply a wood board, with a hole or holes (and lids) conveniently sized to accommodate children and adults. Toilet paper rolls were not readily available and catalog pages or newspapers sufficed. It sure was cold in those outhouses during winter! To use the outhouse on winter mornings, at school or at home, we tried to wait as long as possible, hoping it would warm up outside.

The Sleepy Hollow School was just down the road and up over a big hill, about 20 minutes walking distance from our house. One morning in early autumn, my brother John started walking to school a short distance ahead of my brother Cyril and me. When John was about halfway up the hill, I noticed a large grey wolf walking along the ridge of the hill, toward John. Cyril and I let out a screaming war whoop. John turned toward us in wonderment and simultaneously the wolf hesitated momentarily. In the next instant, the wolf turned and sauntered off toward the nearby woods. We all continued on to school, with no further wolf sightings that day.

About a week or so later, as we sat down to eat supper, we all heard a commotion from the direction of the barnyard and cattle-pen area. The cows and horses were in a panic, the chickens, turkeys and our domestic rabbits scattered every which way and the dogs all barked as never before. Dad grabbed his trusty old 30-30 rifle, maneuvered around the barn, and as he slowly approached the cow pen, he observed a big grey wolf stalking a young calf. The mother cow was snorting and lunging at the wolf. All this action really spooked all the other farm animals. As dad got close enough to clearly see the wolf, he took a steady aim, fired and killed the wolf with a single shot. That wolf then became a living room trophy wolf skin rug until it was destroyed when our house in Herbster, Wisconsin burned down years later in 1934.

Dad believed that the wolf he shot was probably the same one that we had seen stalking John on the way to school. Although we never saw any more wolves on the way to school or near our farm, we knew that wolves were still present in the hilly wooded areas around our farm, because we often listened to them howling from surrounding hilltops, especially on quiet moonlit summer nights.

During the winter of 1924-25, mom and dad decided to hold public barn dances in our big red barn, in order to earn some needed cash to offset our cost of moving around so much. Mom played the piano and dad's musical talent was legendary. His favorite instruments were the violin and mandolin, however, it was widely believed he could play any stringed instrument. With such a reputation, he was once challenged to make music from string (twine) tied between two fence posts. The story has it that he actually did play a tune on that tightened string.

The hay mow (loft) in our big red barn measured about 50 by 80 feet, perfect for a barn dance. Dad constructed an outside stairway up to the large hay loft and the men in the neighborhood helped move our piano into the loft.

Mom and dad practiced and learned the dance tunes of the day, with mom playing the piano and dad the violin and mandolin. Then they advertised their first barn dance which was a big hit and a financial success. My folks continued holding dances about twice a month throughout that winter and spring.

Sometimes, two of dad's brothers, Jim and Frank, joined them at the barn dances with their violins and guitars. The group played music for square dances, fox trots and waltzes. Dad often did the square dance calls and occasionally performed a soft shoe Irish jig.

Young and old couples from the surrounding community came to the barn dances. Local farm wives donated cakes, pies and cookies and some of those women would also bring their babies and children to the dances. On dance nights, our house was filled wall-to-wall with babies and toddlers. Neighborhood grandmothers and mothers would help out by babysitting the small children and preparing sandwiches, desserts and refreshments for sale at the dance. Those volunteers always seemed to be having a great time gossiping about the escapades of the neighbors in the community.

The barn dances were so successful that my folks were able to make up their losses from the move and also purchase a used 1922 Model T Ford. It was our first car, not to mention it being the first one ever in our small rural area.

By the time I was in high school, it became obvious to me that the horse was gradually being replaced by the automobile and the tractor. The signs reading, "Blow Horn Before Entering," that were posted at the city limits of most towns when I was a young boy, were disappearing. Yes, the era of the horse as man's most prized possession and daily transportation, was slowly but surely coming to an end. To say the least, I actually do miss the horse and buggy rides of my youth, as well as the times when I watched our horses running free in the pasture, plowing the fields, or pulling a cultivator through row crops, and then, at harvest time, watching the horses pulling wagons full of farm produce off to market.

A HAPPY MOVE

IN THE SPRING OF 1925, there was good news and bad news for us kids. The bad news — moving again. The good news-- we would be moving to a better farm with a better school. We would be leaving behind our isolated hilly farm with poor soil and Sleepy Hollow School, to a low land farm with richer soil and better equipped one-room school.

Really, none of us kids were able to adjust to the small one-room Sleepy Hollow School for that year, or the isolation of being several miles from the nearest town. We had been unaware that mom and dad spent considerable time over the winter searching for a better farm to rent.

The new farm was called the Hoffman farm and was on the other side of Merrill. As things progressed, dad and my older brothers, Lyle, Norbert and Robert started moving the machinery and farm equipment to the Hoffman farm in early April. In May, they began moving the livestock and other farm animals and started the spring planting. The last week in May, school was out and, we all were passed into the next grades. That weekend, we moved all the household furniture into the Hoffman farm house.

All of us kids were ready for a summer vacation and new adventures on the new farm. It did not take long to find a few swimming holes on the clear water, sandy bottom creek that ran across the farm only a short distance from the house. The old swimming hole was great--sans swim suits for the boys. Our favorite water sport was watering down the dirt bank slope and sliding into the water below.

One day our blind workhorse, Dewey, stumbled over the

edge of the bank and fell about ten or so feet into the creek bed below. He landed on an old abandoned single steel blade from a one-horse walking plow. The blade cut a gash about one foot long on his belly. Dad, being the typical self-sufficient farmer that he was, came to the rescue. He put a halter on Dewey and led him into the clear water, washed the wound and medicated it. Using a curved upholstery needle, he sewed up the huge gash and led Dewey out of the creek and to a fenced-in pasture separated from the creek.

Most farmers would have shot a horse that badly injured. Good old faithful and blind Dewey did fully recover and continued working as a draft horse. However, about a year later Dewey died while pulling a two row com cultivator with two other horses. Dad removed Dewey's harness and drove the other two horses back to the barn. Then he returned with a shovel and buried Dewey where he fell, in that cornfield, pulling his burden to the very end.

Life on the new farm continued much the same as before. Springtime was for planting crops, summer was for cultivating and autumn was the start of school with crop harvesting well under way--a very busy time of year. Everyone in the family who was old enough, or big enough, pitched in and helped with whatever he or she was capable of doing. Sometimes, I would get up around 6:00 A.M. to help my older brothers round up the milk cows and herd them into the milking barn. To do this, I had to go through dew-soaked brush and tall weeds. How I hated that job! Of course, I helped with many other chores during the day, such as gathering the eggs, feeding the poultry, occasionally helping with the milking, picking vegetables and, the job I really liked, picking strawberries.

During that first summer on the Hoffman farm, my oldest brother, Lyle, broke an arm and the other one a few days later. Lyle had been really enjoying summer vacation, as were all of us. But, for some reason or another, Lyle always seemed more vigorous, energetic and aggressive than the rest of us, both in chores and games. One day while riding one of our three ponies, Lyle decided to race a few of the neighbor kids who were also on ponies. I can still visualize them. Someone yelled "Go!" and off they all went, down the dirt road, like a shot out of a cannon, in a cloud of dust. When the dust cleared, there were two riderless ponies on the side of the road and two dusty, scratched-up boys lying on the road moaning. Lyle broke an arm, the other boy ended up with a sprained ankle.

That was not the end of the story. About a week before the cast was to be removed, Lyle, standing near a windmill powered water well pump, got the shirt sleeve of his free arm caught in a huge cog wheel of the equipment. His arm went between the cogs which finally stopped the machine. Dad had to remove one of the cog wheels to get Lyle's arm out. Result-- a severely chewed, mangled, broken arm, and now both arms in a sling. What a way to spend summer vacation!

That first summer on the Hoffman Farm was great fun, but, it ended too soon and it was time to start school again, September, 1925, me in fourth grade at the Merrill School. The new school was too far away to walk, so, again we went to school in our own one-horse buggy, always carrying a big water bucket and a bale of hay and grain for the horse.

School started at 9:00 a.m. and ended at 4:00 p.m. I can still remember how, during the winter time, it would get really cold riding in the buggy. Mom knew how to solve that problem, it was back to warming bricks to keep our feet warm. We still had the old black bearskin blanket and, when the weather was really cold, we would all huddle underneath it like a bunch of chicks underneath the mother hen.

The new school was indeed larger and much better equipped than the Sleepy Hollow school. It had a side room with an inside water pump and a kitchen sink. The wood-burning stove was equipped with a flame control device. Each student had an individual oak desk with an attached seat. However, the toilet was still an outside privy with the usual hole in a wood board seat, with the familiar and reliable Sears-

Roebuck catalog always handy, for reading, too, of course.

Esther Anna Tobin, a city girl who had recently graduated from college, was appointed as our teacher that year. I guess I still remember her name because she was so very special, she was well liked by all and seemed to fit well into the rural community. In fact, I found out years later that, after teaching there for a few years, she married a local farmer who owned a farm only a few miles from the school.

That school year, nothing unusual or great happened and at the end of the school year, we all were passed into the next grades and looked happily forward to the 1926 summer vacation.

A FAMILY PET GOOSE NAMED GOZZY

OCCASIONALLY, WHEN I THINK ABOUT the time when we lived on the Hoffman farm, my thoughts turn to our special pet goose. A neighbor, who raised geese for market, gave us kids a just hatched little gosling. We named him Gozzy. That fuzzy little gosling got more attention than any of our pet dogs ever did. Eventually, he became our pampered, overfed pet.

The gosling probably thought we kids were its parents and became very attached and bonded to each of us. Whenever we were in the yard, he would follow us around, even joining us in games and swimming in the nearby creek. He loved to beg for grains. The more we fed him, the more he grew, and the more he grew the more we fed him. By the time we started school in September, Gozzy was a full grown gander and the biggest goose in our farming area.

Each day as we returned from school, that goose would often beat our dog Turk to greet us at the gate and follow us to the house. He would stay in the yard and play with us until supper time. Then, when we went into the house, he would retreat to a special place he claimed for himself in the barn.

That autumn in 1925, dad seemed to make a special point of showing us kids a porker and calf that he was fattening for Thanksgiving. When we sat down for what we expected to be a happy Thanksgiving meal, we had the shock of our life! There on the table were an expected roasted porker, a beef rib roast and an unexpected big, fat roasted goose! We kids all gasped in disbelief. I ran to the window, no goose to be seen! I ran outside in a panic, calling for Gozzy, but, there was no sign of our pet goose. I returned to the table and asked dad straight out, "Did you kill Gozzy?" Not a word from anyone.

At that, all of us kids left the table, unable to eat anything. Dad finally took the cooked goose to a nearby neighbor, who happily accepted the offering. But it took mom hours to persuade us to eat the now cold pork and beef Thanksgiving dinner, minus the family pet goose.

Never again did dad slaughter (for us kids) any farm animal that became a family pet. I believe that the experience affected dad much worse than it did us kids. He spent the next several months doing all kinds of favors for us kids, hoping that we would soon forget the ordeal. However, we kids really never forgot the fate that befell our special pet Gozzy.

MOVING AGAIN

WHEN SUMMER VACATION in 1926 came to an end, we were all back in school, me in fifth grade. As expected, school was going fine and all seemed well. However, even though everything on the Hoffman farm and at the Merrill School was a great improvement over the hill country farm and the Sleepy Hollow School, it was still significantly more isolated than we were accustomed to. None of us children really adjusted to that sort of isolated rural life.

Early in December, in preparation for the holidays, mom and dad went shopping in the nearby town of Le Mars. While shopping for hardware items at the Le Mars Hardware-Lumberyard, dad noticed a sign "Carpenter/Handyman Wanted." The pay included a rent free five-bedroom house located across the street. Dad applied for the job and was hired to start full time work within three months, in March, 1927.

What a frantic winter that turned into preparing for the move. We held a public auction in January to sell everything, including all the farm equipment, machinery and farm animals. In February, we moved into the 5 bedroom house, a few weeks before dad's new job started.

That city house was a pleasant and luxurious change from the previous farm houses that we lived in. The city house had a covered porch which extended almost halfway around the house. One part of it was shady in the morning, the other part in the afternoon. What a nice place to sit in the swing seat and relax. More importantly, it had an inside bathroom with a flush toilet and bath tub, hot and cold running water, five large bedrooms, a telephone and electric lights.

In contrast to our new home, all of the farm houses that we had lived in prior had only outside privy's (no indoor plumbing). Kitchen hot water was supplied from a reservoir tank connected to the kitchen stove, which we filled from the outside water pump. Those other farm houses had a makeshift bathtub, which was a round 20 gallon metal clothes wash-tub, that we dragged into the kitchen on Saturdays for our weekly baths. In the summer time, you had the option of taking a bath in the creek. Saturday night on the farm had always been bath night, had to be nice and clean for church on Sunday morning.

The St. Joseph Catholic School (grades 1-12) was about 10 to 15 minutes walking distance from our house. About 300 students attended St. Joseph. The school had inside toilets, two each for the boys and girls, and not a Sears catalog in any of them, only rolls of toilet paper.

We started school about mid-March, 1927. The principal recommended that I complete fifth grade, but repeat it again the following year. Her reasoning was that because of all our previous moves, my illnesses, and changes of schools, I had missed too many school days.

After the school year ended, during vacation that summer of 1927, my friend and classmate, Lowell Luken, convinced me to sign up for beginner swimming class with him. The swimming classes were held at a lake which had been formed years earlier when workers dug into an underground aquifer when mining an open mined gravel pit. The water rushed into the excavated areas and created a man made lake about ten acres in size, big enough for the City of Lemars to develop into a municipal recreation center.

One day after swimming class, I was dog paddling in the pool and drifted into deep water. When I realized that I couldn't touch the bottom, I accelerated my dog paddle and headed for the shallow part of the pool. I paddled furiously, but was making little progress. I was getting tired and out of breath as I floundered in the water. I tried to yell for help as I struggled to stay afloat. Soon I reached the panic stage and began gulping water while gasping for air.

A good swimmer recognized my plight, and rushed to my aid. When he reached me, he grabbed my arm and pulled me to shore. Later, I was told that my body was turning blue and I had stopped breathing. The lifeguard had taken charge immediately, he turned me on my belly and began resuscitation efforts. He systematically pushed the water out of my lungs and breathed air in. Soon, I was sitting up, pale-faced and embarrassed.

I never told my parents about the ordeal, but I did continue with swimming classes and was a very attentive student. Within a couple of weeks, I advanced to the intermediate level, and by the end of summer, I had attained the qualified swimmers' level.

NEIGHBORHOOD BULLIES
AND SCHOOL CONFLICTS

THE RELATIVELY SHORT WALK to school from our house in LeMars took us kids by an apartment complex where several public school children lived when I was in 6th grade at St. Joseph's Catholic School. Our older brothers, Norbert and Robert, usually walked together to and from school at a different time than Cyril, John and I.

Occasionally, some of the apartment boys would hassle me and my younger brothers, Cyril and John. For some reason or other, they never paid any attention to any of the girls (little or big). They would taunt us with remarks like, "Kids who go to St. Joseph are sissies and have to pray all day."

Soon, the taunting from the apartment boys escalated into pushing us off the sidewalk. Of course, we weren't as tough as they were, so we started walking on the other side of the street to avoid them. The bullies (always just a little bigger than us) weren't satisfied to leave us alone, they followed us to the other side of the street to continue their bad behavior. Of course, this only happened when no adults were present.

Then one day, on our way home from school, it happened that my younger brothers were walking a short distance ahead of me. We were walking across the street from the apartment, wanting to avoid any confrontation with the bullies. As we walked along, I saw three young boys run across the street and push my brothers off the sidewalk, then, they ran off laughing. At home that evening, my younger brothers and I told our bigger brothers, Norbert and Robert, what had happened. The five of us planned our strategic counter offensive.

On our way home, the five of us planned to go home at the same time, but we would stagger our positions far enough apart so that the youngest three would appear to be alone (those apartment house bullies had no idea that we were a family of eight boys and two girls). The two oldest, Norbert and Robert, would take up the lead and the rear guard positions, respectively. They were to walk on the apartment side of the street, while Cyril, John and I would be the bait, across the street, walking alone a few feet apart from each other.

We implemented our plan each day, always being vigilant. Then one day it happened, five of the bullies (three big boys and two smaller ones) spotted me, Cyril and John spread out and just moseying along across the street from the apartments. They hurried across the street and headed straight for Cyril and John, the youngest of us. Before they knew what hit them, the three big ones were targeted by Norbert and Robert. Cyril and I grabbed the two smallest ones.

It was swift poetic justice, Norbert banged two heads together, Robert tackled his mark, and our little brother John took turns punching the boys that Cyril and I held. As those bullies broke away, one by one, they scurried away (like scared rabbits), back to their apartment premises. As they ran off, Norbert and Robert shouted at them, "If you sissies want more of the same, there are still five more of us at home!" After that fiasco, they never taunted us again, no matter which side of the street we walked on.

In January, 1930, I transferred in the middle of my seventh grade year from St. Joseph's Catholic School to the LeMars Central Public School. Cyril and John followed. Ironically, after switching to their school, some of those apartment gang of boys were in classes with me, Cyril and John, and some eventually became good friends. Often, on weekends, holidays and summertime, they played basketball, baseball and other games with us and other kids from the neighborhood, in a public park near our home.

My mid-year transfer in seventh grade, from St. Joseph Catholic School to Le Mars Central public school, was the result of a confrontation with one of the nuns at the school, she was my language and writing teacher. From the beginning of school, she seemed to enjoy picking on a few of the students, including me and two of my best friends, Lowell Luken and Marcella Schultz. She frequently made remarks that embarrassed us in front of the other students, making comments like "your homework is too messy to accept, you dress funny, and where did you find such clothes."

There was a good reason for the clothes I wore, the Great Depression of 1929 was wide spread across the country and many heads of households were unemployed. Dad was unemployed intermittently, and sometimes had only part time work during the depression. We couldn't afford any expensive clothing, and what we did have was mostly hand me downs or used clothing from friends or welfare.

A few days before the 1929 Christmas vacation, my class was practicing the Palmer method of penmanship, writing in script. The teacher, walking up and down between the row of desks, carrying a ruler, keenly inspecting each one's writing. When she reached my desk, she accused me of being deliberately messy. Then, all of a sudden, WHAM, BAM, she whacked me across the back of my hand with the edge of that wooden ruler. Ouch! Did that ever hurt!

But that wasn't the end of it. Before she moved on, she warned me that she would return to check my work again at the end of class. Only moments later, my two friends got the same treatment. When she returned to my desk, I was too nervous to do better than a real messy and shaky scribble. That merited another whack, this time across my fingers. Aie, yhi, eee, that smarted and brought tears to my eyes. Then she said, "you're too messy for words!" Just then the bell rang and class ended. Literally, I was saved by the bell. I exited the room, embarrassed and stunned, with a shattered ego. Like my dad before me, my handwriting was then, and still is, barely legible.

Since writing class was weekly, on Wednesday, I had plenty of time to decide what recourse I would take. By Friday, the last school day before Christmas vacation, my mind was made up. I would show my objection to the teacher's antics with my feet. At the end of classes, I gathered my books and school supplies and walked out of the school, with plans not to return, but to transfer to Central public school.

On the way home that day, my friends Lowell and Marcella and I discussed our dismay and dilemma. They both thought about being sick every Wednesday in order to miss the penmanship class. Not wanting to reveal my plans, I agreed that maybe their idea would work, at least temporarily. I hurried home in anticipation of a happy two weeks vacation.

On the first day of school in January, 1930, I left home earlier than the others and instead of going to school at St. Joseph, I went directly to the Principal's office at Central, the public school. The Principal asked why my parents didn't accompany me with my report card. I explained they were unable to and that I would take care of things. The Principal said that he would contact St. Joseph's school to confirm my grade status. He entered my name on the school enrollment roster and then accompanied me to what was to become my home room for the remainder of the seventh grade. Word soon got out to my former classmates that I had jumped ship. My mom, in turn received a hostile phone call from the Principal of St. Joseph's, wanting to know why she enrolled me in Central.

Upon my return home from my first day at Central Public School, mom confronted me at the front door with a, "Well, how was school today and don't pretend that you don't know what I mean." Nonchalantly, I said, "Oh, I forgot to tell you, I'm now going to the public school." Of course, that evoked a short but vigorous discussion. After I explained about the treatment that had been meted out for me and my friends, she was sympathetic to my plight. She promised to let me remain in public school.

The following morning, mom went to St. Joseph to discuss my treatment with the principal. My writing teacher made light of the incident and the principal was reluctant to discuss the matter, since I had already enrolled at Central. Mom and dad were disappointed with the principal's lack of concern for the students. The very next day, on Wednesday, mom enrolled my three brothers (Robert, Cyril and John) and two sisters (Margaret and Catherine) at Central. She didn't enroll Norbert, because over Christmas vacation Norbert found a job and dropped out of school.

The next week, my two close friends, Lowell and Marcella, also left St. Joseph's and enrolled at Central, both were assigned to my home room. By the end of that week, three more seventh graders (2 boys and 1 girl) from St. Joseph's had enrolled at Central and were also assigned to my home room. Within two weeks after I had jumped ship, a total of eleven students, including six from my family, had transferred to Central.

The sudden exodus caused quite a stir in the parish. The Pastor and the School Board initiated an investigation. The findings resulted in the writing teacher being reassigned to a clerical job at the large parish hospital. According to my friends, things returned to normal at St. Joseph Catholic School after the writing teacher was removed.

Not that public school was without issues. A few weeks after entering Central Public School, I found my little brother Stephen (who was in first grade at the time) standing and crying in the hallway outside his classroom. I asked him why he was in the hallway during class time. He said that he didn't know why, but that the teacher had just told him to leave the room and stand in the hall until the class ended.

After my own humiliating experience at the hands of the writing teacher in seventh grade, I was not about to stand by and let my brother be similarly treated. I went directly to the Central School Principal and asked him for help. I also told him that I was going to tell my mom about it. The Principal accompanied me to where Stephen was and found him still crying. The Principal asked him why he was in the hallway. Again, Stephen said he didn't know why. The Principal called his teacher into the hall and asked her for an explanation. She simply replied, "because he was inattentive during class instructions."

The principal told Stephen to return to his desk, and followed up with an investigation of the teacher's practices. Having had several complaints from other parents, the teacher, who was a recent college graduate on her first teaching assignment, was summarily dismissed by the school board for incompetence, with less than one month remaining in her first semester on the job.

I recall my mother's standard explanation for people who behave badly, "Just remember, there is good and bad among all." Like my mother, I acknowledge the premise that good and bad coexists in all people and the institutions, organizations or other groupings that they belong to, including educational, religious, civic, political, charitable, professional or otherwise. I might add that, except for teachers like my ruler-wacking teacher and the public school teacher who made my brother stand in the hall for no good reason, I have the highest respect and praise for the dedication of my teachers. I may have disliked the peculiar antics of some individual administrators, staff or teachers, but not the fundamental policies, regulations and rules of the institutions which employed them.

My experience with that ruler-wacking seventh grade teacher had a dramatic negative impact upon my psyche. In the school years that followed, my interest in school and studying suffered a temporary decline and I became somewhat withdrawn socially. That negative school experience definitely created within me a strong dislike for mean-spirited, arrogant, sarcastic persons, especially those who abuse the authority entrusted to them. I instinctively became a lifelong advocate for fairness and concern for the underdog.

It wasn't until ninth and tenth grades, with much encouragement from my buddies, Lowell and Marcella, and my new friends at Central, that I began to emerge from that shell of a negative and indifferent attitude toward school. I began accompanying my friends to football games, basketball games and eventually to school parties in tenth grade.

My siblings and I remained at Central Public School until June, 1933, and in the summer, we moved to Herbster, Wisconsin, where I was enrolled in the 11th grade of high school.

PART 3

THE GREAT DEPRESSION
OF 1929

STATE OF THE UNION

IN THE PRESIDENTIAL CAMPAIGN OF 1928, Alfred E. Smith, a Democrat, ran against Herbert Hoover, a Republican. Hoover won and what followed is now recorded history of wrong decisions and failed policies leading to the national financial crisis and the stock market crash in October 19, 1929 (known as Black Tuesday), which set off an unprecedented and devastating economic crisis throughout the entire United States known as the Great Depression. Unemployment in the U.S. rose to 25 percent and had devastating effects worldwide. Farming and rural areas suffered as crop prices fell by approximately 60 percent. Some economies started to recover by the mid-1930s.

Franklin D. Roosevelt, a Democrat, won the following Presidential election by a landslide in 1932 against the incumbent, one-term President Herbert Hoover, a Republican. Roosevelt ran on a platform called the "New Deal", promising a more active Federal role to combat the devastation and financial chaos of the Great Depression. President Roosevelt appointed many professors to his new Cabinet, for which it was aptly dubbed The Brain Trust.

President Roosevelt and his Cabinet of intellectuals focused on solving the financial crisis inherited from the Hoover Administration, including unemployment, falling prices, failed banks, bankruptcies and general financial chaos. In a bold action to combat the Great Depression, the President implemented a plan to stabilize prices, abolish child labor and ensure collective bargaining for labor. Called the National Industrial Recovery Act of 1933, it appropriated $3.3 billion for public works projects to prime the pump of declining business enterprise.

To manage the appropriation, the Act established the Works Program Administration (WPA). It also created the Civilian Conservation Corps (CCC) which was a quasi-military program centrally organized at military bases, and utilizing resources of Federal and State agencies responsible for forestry management. The CCC carried out a national reforestation program, employing men within the ages of 18 to 36, to plant trees and build access roads and bridges as needed.

Never did I think that I would live to witness anything like the Great Depression again. Now, some 80 years later, at the age of 97, I am witnessing a repeat of history, commencing with the economic crisis in the first part of this 21st century, rampant with corporate and personal greed, insufficient financial regulation, massive unemployment, increased rate of bankruptcies, healthcare crisis, a widening gap in the distribution of wealth and amplified political divisiveness. To make things worse, the world is faced with outpaced industrial age pollution, nuclear facility disasters and global warming.

In the 2008 Presidential election, after two terms served by President George W. Bush, the Democratic candidate Barack H. Obama was elected president over Senator John M. McCain, the Republican candidate. Like President Roosevelt, who inherited the Hoover economic crisis when he took office in 1932, President Obama inherited the Bush economic crisis of 2008. It took Roosevelt more than 10 years to stabilize the economy after the Great Depression of 1929, and recorded history will tell if Obama satisfactorily met the challenge as did Roosevelt.

ECONOMIC DISASTER

LIKE SO MANY OTHER FAMILIES in our community, we too, were affected by the Great Depression of 1929. Money for loans became almost nonexistent, jobs were even scarcer. Simultaneously, as unemployment skyrocketed, the price of commodities plummeted, triggering a dramatic chain reaction of continuing layoffs across America. Health care and welfare assistance was not available to properly care for the thousands of unemployed. The unemployed couldn't afford to buy things, so production was reduced, causing more layoffs of workers in manufacturing plants. The situation went from bad to worse, like a tornado destroying everything in its path, including dreams and hope.

In February, 1930, the lumberyard where my dad worked for 3 years, went bankrupt and he joined the ranks of the unemployed. The house we lived in was sold at auction along with the lumberyard business. The new owner agreed to let us stay in the house until dad found work, not to exceed six months. With dad unemployed, no one would rent a house to him. About four months later, dad was hired part-time at a heating fuel company (wood, coal and oil). Though we lived rent-free for those four months while dad looked for other work, what little money my folks had saved was quickly exhausted on food and utilities.

After dad found a part time job, he was able to rent a house and plant a large garden. However, even though dad now had some regular income, we were still in a desperate situation. Dad's part time paycheck was barely enough to pay for rent and utilities, with a mere pittance remaining for food and other necessities and the garden wouldn't yield any crop until autumn. Eventually, the day came when we had no money or food and no credit left at the grocery store. The only food in the house was field picked dandelion greens for salad and potatoes with gravy made from bacon grease, and only enough for supper that night. After that meal, we knew that there was no food left for the next day except free for the picking of dandelions' and lambs' quarters greens. An uninvited guest, the Great Depression, had truly arrived at our home.

I can still vividly remember sitting down for that meal of only cooked potatoes, gravy and dandelion greens. My father said Grace, "Let us pray and thank the Lord for this food." My mother followed that with, "Yes, we thank you Lord for this food, especially knowing that some of our friends may even have less." Dad left before any of us got up the following morning and drove from farm to farm seeking food in exchange for work. After talking to at least five or six farmers, he found one who needed some help, but he could only pay in eggs. Dad arrived home just before supper time with a thirty dozen crate of fresh eggs. He traded some of the eggs with a neighbor for potatoes and other vegetables. That night for supper, we had all the eggs we could eat plus potatoes, carrots, onions, tomatoes and a dandelion salad, but no bread or milk.

In the days that followed, dad continued offering work for food on the nearby farms. After each trip, he would come home with at least one food item, but usually he earned an assortment of farm foods like chickens, corn-on-the-cob, grains for flour, squash, cabbage, onions, tomatoes, potatoes, melons or whatever other food the farmers might have in exchange for dad's labor.

At the height of the Depression, the government (federal, state and local),established food surplus distribution centers across the nation. Soon to follow, private and religious organizations opened soup kitchens and housing units to care for the homeless, often whole families. Many locally owned butcher shops gave fat and bone scraps free to the unemployed for soup. The scraps had previously been sold to rendering plants to be processed into grease and dog foods.

If I remember correctly, day old bread cost a nickel a loaf (3 for a dime), whole milk cost a nickel a quart (skimmed was a nickel per gallon), vegetables cost only pennies per pound or bunch, meats were only pennies per pound, fat and bone scraps were free for the asking. There's no doubt about it, those soup kitchens, government surplus foods, the fat and bone scraps and nature's greens actually saved the lives of many of the unemployed workers and their families.

For quite sometime after that supper of only dandelion salad, potatoes and gravy, our dinner and supper meals consisted of what we called "Depression Soup." It was made with free fat trimmings and stripped meat bones from the local butcher shop and any other meat or vegetables that dad gathered from the farms he visited regularly, on a work for food agreement. The fat and bone scraps saved us from what would have otherwise been a starvation diet.

After several months of offering work for food among the farmers, dad was hired full time at the heating fuel company. We had survived the worst, thanks to dad and the generosity of some farmers. By autumn of 1932, with a bumper crop from our big garden, a big apple tree full of fruit and dad gainfully employed full time, our lives returned to normal and the future looked promising.

MY MOM'S
DEPRESSION SOUP RECIPE

Ingredients

bones and fat

stripped bones & fat trimmings
(the local butcher shop provided them
at no cost, if you were poor or unemployed)

vegetables

any vegetables you get your hands on
(your own crop, and/or beg, borrow, or trade)

seasonings

salt, pepper, add herbs if available

Directions

Place bones and fat in a large pot of water, bring to a boil, and simmer for about one hour. Remove bones and fat scraps from the broth. Skim the grease from the top of the soup and reserve it for making soap later.

Return to the broth all bone marrow obtained from cracking the bones open, and any residual meat that could be pulled from the bones and scraps.

Add the vegetables and seasonings to taste and simmer until the vegetables are tender. Don't discard anything, give fat scraps and cooked bones to your hungry dog or cat and reserve any grease to make soap later.

Optional

If fortunate enough to have a spare dime, mom added skimmed milk and bread to the meal. Whole milk was five cents per quart, but for the same amount you could buy a whole gallon of skimmed milk. Bread sold for five cents a loaf, or three for 10 cents.

TEENAGERS PITCHED IN

TEENAGERS HELPED their families financially as best they could. For example, early in the summer of 1930, my brother Cyril and I started caddying at the Le Mars Golf Country Club and our brother John started the following year. After saving our earnings for about one month, we bought a second hand lawnmower. Soon, we were mowing lawns in the neighborhood. When not mowing lawns, we would go to the golf course to caddy. By September, Cyril and I had enough money saved to buy some school clothes and put aside a little reserve for school items needed later, and a little for mom for groceries.

In late summer 1930, with lawn mowing and caddying about finished for the season, Cyril and I got jobs delivering a newspaper, the Sioux City Journal. Each evening after school, we made home deliveries. Then, we would both go downtown and sell papers at the hotel and restaurants for about another hour. Though the depression still lingered on, tips were generally pretty good.

I especially enjoyed hawking the newspapers in one special restaurant. The owner was a kind and friendly lady. After only a few days of offering the papers for sale to her customers, the weather turned cold and snowy. As I sat by the front door looking out into the cold night, she tapped me on the shoulder and asked, "Young man, would you like a nice bowl of hot soup?" I guess she noticed how fast I ate the soup. She then asked, "Do you suppose you could find room for a sandwich and a glass of milk?" I will never forget that lady. She refused my offer to pay (the change in my pocket would not have covered the bill). She talked with me about my family, my plans for schooling, etc. For the remainder of the time that I had that paper route, a sandwich, a glass of milk and a slice of pie, was the offer of the day, no charge. I have never forgotten her kindness. My lasting impression of the depression was that it brought out the best in many people. There seemed to have been a sincere display of kindness and concern for others in need.

The paper route turned out to be a good winter job and it provided us with sufficient funds for our school activities. Also, the money we earned was occasionally given to our parents to help through rough times when dad was employed part time.

One day, when delivering the paper to a neighbor who had three young boys, I was asked if I would give them haircuts. She offered to teach me the basics of barbering and give me one of the two clippers she had in exchange for cutting her children's hair. So, I took up the offer and started practicing on her three kids and my younger brothers. After a few haircuts, I actually did pretty well. By the start of school in 1931, I was a good enough barber to give all those going to school a really first-class-off-to-school type haircut. From then on, I became the official unpaid barber for the kids in our family and some of the neighbor's kids.

MAKING THE BEST
OF A BAD SITUATION

IN SPITE OF THE GREAT DEPRESSION, while living in LeMars, Iowa, I have many fond recollections of the almost six years we lived there, especially the summer vacations. During that time, the population of the city was about five thousand. Our home, on the east side of the city, was only a short distance from the municipal public recreation park. The park was situated on the shore of two large man-made lakes (former gravel pits) just outside of the city. The park provided many amenities and leisure activities for the public such as: swimming, rowing, concessions, restaurants, grassy areas for sports, children's playgrounds, picnic areas and public toilets.

On holidays and special civic events, whole families would gather in the park to celebrate the occasion. It was customary then to prepare a picnic lunch for the outing. At meal time, families would share their food with each other, very much like present day "Pot Luck" parties.

The city of Le Mars also had a large public park in the center of the city (near Central Public School) appropriately named Central Park. That park also had a picnic area, a playground for kids and a large gazebo to accommodate all types of summer civic events, such as: musical performances, political rallies and social gatherings.

On Saturday afternoons and evenings (in the summertime) musical performances were provided free for the public. During the mid afternoon, a band would play military marching music. The band was mostly composed of local young American men of German heritage, dressed in attractive multicolored uniforms. A large crowd always turned out for their performances. Later on, in the cool of the evening, about 7 p.m., the German band would be replaced by a group of local musicians. Those musicians would play dance music and popular songs until about 10 p.m. When they played popular music, many couples would sit on the grass surrounding the gazebo, while others danced on the adjacent large platform.

In the nearby town of Akron, the 4th of July was always the big celebration of the summer. Main Street would be closed to traffic and filled with booths for hot foods, souvenirs and carnival games. Every year, the main attraction was free watermelon, served from noon until sunset, then the crowd moved to a park on the edge of town, for the exciting display of fireworks.

When I was a teenager, there were no public organized summertime sports or recreational programs for the school children, at least not in our community. What to do! Well, on our own initiative, we kids organized our own neighborhood activities, a Charlie Brown type of softball, basketball, etc. Having no rule book, we developed our own rules as summer progressed, and, having no gymnasium, we played our games in the neighborhood vacant lot. Each year I was first baseman on the softball team and right guard on the basketball team. In 1932, our softball team won all of its games and we became the city champs. We were rewarded with a team photograph, a blurb in the local town bulletin and great notoriety in the local community.

When I was 16 to 18 years old, from 1931 to 1933, I was a caddy at the Le Mars Country Club golf course. During slow days at the golf course, I would borrow some clubs and play a few holes until someone needed me to caddy. Eventually, I developed a pretty good swing and played well enough to win the caddy's tournament for three consecutive years, 1931, 1932 and 1933.

Age 16

The last year I caddied, in the summer of 1933, my tournament score was 126 for 36 holes, six under par (par was 66 for 18 holes). Incidentally, a young man named Wernly, who I beat each of those three years, won the Iowa State Amateur Tournament in 1934. Having no clubs of my own, I borrowed some for each of the three tournaments I competed in. The first prize in the 1933 tournament was a golf bag and a full set of clubs. Finally, I had clubs of my own and could practice any time I wanted. Unfortunately, in August, 1933, our family moved to a farm in northern Wisconsin, a farming, lumbering and fishing community with no golf course anywhere nearby.

I loved basketball in those days as much as golf. When I was about 16 years old, while still living in Le Mars, the Harlem Globetrotters gave a benefit basketball performance at our local high school gymnasium. Out of curiosity, I went to the school to get a look at the famous professional basketball team.

There I was, standing near the entrance to the gymnasium just before game time, when the team arrived and started to enter the gym. One team member, more than 6 feet tall, waved and asked, "You watching the game tonight?" "No," I said, "I don't have enough money for a ticket." Then he said, "Here, carry one of my bags and just say nothing but follow me." Off we went, then he told me that in case anyone asked, to let him do the talking--no problem. They played our best local team and what a beating our team took. I thought it was nice of them to let our team make a basket occasionally. I never saw the Globetrotters play again, except in the movies or on T.V.

Those were adventurous years. We did some very exciting and sometimes dumb things. When I was about 16 years old and Cyril was 15, we got permission from mom and dad to hitchhike to Remsen, only a few miles away, to visit a friend who formerly attended our school in LeMars. On the way to the highway to hitchhike, a freight train came by going slow enough to hop on. As it turned out, the train was going west instead of north. So, we decided to go on a sight-seeing trip.

The next day, we found ourselves passing through the western part of South Dakota. When we had gone as far as Montana, we sent a post card telling our folks that we hoped to be home in a few days. A few days later we did make our way back home. We had a great time on that adventure and saw an awful lot of the Midwestern states, hobo style. When we arrived home, we found out that our folks had been just worried sick about us. Kids can sure do some dumb things, huh?

After having personally observed three separate generations of children growing up (my siblings, my children and my grandchildren), I have come to believe that almost all persons, when young children, don't realize or understand just how much their parents love and care for them, until they become adults or have children of their own. It's probably been like that since Adam and Eve's kids and, more than likely, it will continue that way forever.

MOVE TO WISCONSIN

LATE IN THE SUMMER OF 1933, both my father (at age 53) and my brother Norbert (at age 23) found jobs in Herbster, Wisconsin. About the same time, my brother Robert, 20 years old, signed up for two years in the Civilian Conservation Corps (CCC) and was assigned to an army base in northern Iowa.

Before we made the move to Wisconsin, dad made arrangements for the purchase of a 40-acre farm about 3 miles south of the town of Herbster. To make the trip to Wisconsin, dad sold his old model T-Ford and bought a 1931 Model A Ford and a four-wheel auto trailer. Once again, we sold everything except clothing and useful small household items, like pots and pans, that could be packed in the car and trailer. We looked like gypsies or wandering nomads.

I will never forget leaving LeMars, Iowa, and striking out for far away Herbster, Wisconsin, with plans and high hopes for a happier and more prosperous future. It was really sad leaving so many close school friends behind, knowing I would probably never see them again. In fact, I never did see any of them again, but I have not forgotten them, especially Lowell, Marcela, Snooky, Roman, Paul, and Bill.

After one look at the load in the car and the trailer, my brother Cyril and I decided to hitchhike to Herbster, after all, we were seasoned hitchhikers. Dad and my older brother, Norbert, alternated driving the car. With compass in hand, our hitchhike team (Cyril and I) waved goodbye to the car-trailer bunch and both teams set off on course, north toward Wisconsin. As it turned out, Cyril and I, guided by the stars at night and compass by day, arrived in Herbster before the others.

We traveled hobo style, riding on a freight train from Le Mars, Iowa to Minneapolis, Minnesota. Then we hitchhiked in Minnesota from St. Paul to Duluth and on to Superior, Wisconsin before reaching our final destination of Herbster, Wisconsin. At night, we had found places to sleep in train stations, public parks and on roadsides, depending on availability. For nourishment, we stopped at grocery stores and offered work for food. In every case, the storekeepers were very generous and we were never hungry for the entire trip.

At that time, Herbster was a small town of about ten families, about 40 people in all. The town was situated on the south shore of Lake Superior. We arrived at our new home the first week in September, 1933. My first impression was ecstatic, "what a beautiful place!" It was about 3 miles south of Herbster, on the edge of a big forest with a small trout stream, Cranberry Creek, flowing through the property. Because of its location, there were many wild animals roaming everywhere, including deer, black bears, possum, porcupines, skunks, ground hogs, squirrels and many species of birds. About 35 acres of the 40-acre farm were under cultivation, mostly for wheat and hay and including a large vegetable garden spot.

The farm had a nice big 2-story house with an outside hand-operated water well pump, an outhouse, a big machinery storage shed and a car garage. We finally got organized and well prepared for the expected cold winter. We all had new winter clothes, the pantry was full of packages of flour, rice, beans, sugar and canned foods. The trout stream (Cranberry Creek) had an abundance of fish and deer were plentiful in the nearby forest. What more could one ask for?!

The public school in Herbster included grades one through eleven (there was no twelfth grade). School had already started by the time we had finally moved into our new home. We began attending school in September, 1933, just a few days late, me in the eleventh grade. The Herbster school was a nice facility with most of the amenities of big city schools and a motorized school bus picked us up each day for school. We thought that was great, no more horse and buggy problems for us!

Job possibilities in Herbster, an agricultural, lumbering and fishing community, appeared really bleak for me and my teenage brothers. At least, we found none of the types of jobs that we were previously accustomed to in Iowa. Luckily though for me, the closest barber shop was in Port Wing, about ten miles from Herbster, and the price of a haircut was twenty-five cents. I got the word out that students could get a haircut for only a dime, by Christmas vacation, I had trimmed the shaggy manes of several boys from the Herbster school.

My hair clippers, a gift from our neighbor in Le Mars, became a real asset in helping to pay for many of my school expenses during my last two years of high school. During college I continued to benefit from my hair cutting expertise, earning extra pocket change from other students at 25 cents a haircut (uptown price was 50 cents).

Life was looking rosy when tragedy struck early in February, 1934, our first winter in Wisconsin. The house and everything in it burned to the ground, including our winter supply of foods, winter clothes, personal family records, generations of photo albums, furniture, my new set of golf clubs, my bicycle and dad's Stradivarius violin. On the evening of the fire, the temperature had dropped to about 20 below zero degrees F., the coldest temperature recorded so far that winter. Luckily, neighbors saw the flames and billowing smoke and came by to investigate. Thankfully, those good neighbors came to our aid and took us into their homes that night.

The County Social Services provided welcome assistance about two weeks later in the form of emergency food, clothing, furniture and the funds to temporarily rent a large two-story house. The house we rented with those funds was located about one mile east of Herbster on Wisconsin Highway 13. With the help of friends and Social Services, life continued on schedule, and none of us kids missed even a day of school as a result of that unhappy event.

No insurance agents lived in the town of Herbster at that time and communication and travel in the community were still relatively primitive. Unfortunately, due to a sequence of happenstances and rescheduled appointments, the fire struck just a few days before the insurance agent was scheduled to meet with my parents to sign the papers for a previously agreed to fire insurance policy. In those days insurance was not required before purchasing a home.

What a disaster, the only item saved was a walnut writing desk that I had made in tenth grade at Le Mars high school. It was saved only because it was next to the big exit door. By the time my folks tried to re-enter the house, the fire was too intense to retrieve anything else. My folks returned the desk to me on a visit home in 1947, after I got married. When our older son John was married in 1981, we passed the desk on to him.

Eleventh grade was a year of awakening for me. Slowly but progressively, I evolved from a quiet boy into an active teenager. I began raising my hand whenever I knew the answer to the class question or problem. Also, I became involved in extracurricular school activities. I turned out for basketball, joined the debate team and signed up for drama class.

My brothers, Cyril and John, and I played on the Herbster High School basketball team that school year of 1933-34. I was elected High School Prom King for the annual school spring festival and dance. On a more academic note, I participated in the oratory-speech program, was a member of the drama group, and took part in two stage performances sponsored by the high school.

We survived the winter and after school was out that spring of 1934, we moved from the Herbster house into a large log cabin on the Hahn farm, adjacent to our farm. Spring weather was wonderful that year and we planted a very large garden. The summer weather continued to be excellent and we harvested a bumper crop that autumn.

One day early in the summer of 1934, some neighbor kids, my brother Cyril and I were exploring the edge of the forest bordering our farm. I was a little ahead of the others and came face to face with a big black mother bear and two little cubs. Oh yes, it's true--it was no "pooddy cat." After I had time to think about it later, I couldn't understand why that bear didn't take out after me like a raging bull. Well anyway, luckily, it just ran back to its cubs and headed at a slow gallop back into the forest. We all reasoned, on the scene that day, that as soon as the mother bear saw all the others (about 10 of them) not far behind me, she appeared to be more interested in protecting her cubs than in mixing with all of us. Probably, if I had been alone, I could have ended up being dinner for the bear.

In late summer, dad got a job working on the Huxley farm, only a short walking distance from our farm. That job included a house for our family. During August of 1934, the family moved from the log cabin to the much larger house on the Huxley property. I, however, moved to Port Wing to complete the twelfth grade of high school.

In spite of our losses in the house fire, we all bounced back, and I have wonderful memories from that year etched in my mind.

SENIOR YEAR OF HIGH SCHOOL
--THEN COLLEGE

AT THE START OF SUMMER VACATION after completing eleventh grade in Herbster, Gustave Bystrom, the principal and basketball coach at Port Wing High School, contacted me with an offer to complete high school (twelfth grade) at Port Wing, about eight miles west of our home in Herbster. The offer, conditioned upon me joining the basketball team, included a job in the local lumberyard and a small efficiency apartment about one block from school. It was too good to pass up.

On the weekend before school started, I packed my clothes and small belongings in a backpack and hitchhiked to Port Wing. I checked in for the lumberyard job and set up housekeeping in the apartment. On the following Monday morning, I started my last year of high school.

During twelfth grade, 1934-35, whenever I wasn't working or studying, I was in the gym practicing basketball. I played in every scheduled game for the whole season. What a time I had playing basketball my senior year--and no trouble for dates for school programs or local dances. I became a member of the high school drama club and took the lead role in both the junior class and senior class three act plays, "Spooky Tavern" and "Eyes of Love. " I was 20 years old when I graduated at the end of the school year, June, 1935.

Whenever I think about the number of schools I attended from first grade (1921) through twelfth grade (1935), I realize just how often my folks moved around, from farm to farm and job to job. I had actually attended nine different schools from first grade through high school.

Year	Grade	School
1921-22	1st	St. Patrick's Catholic,
1922-23	1st	Akron, IA (repeated grade)
1923-24	2nd	Westfield Public School Westfield, IA
Spring 1924	3rd	Akron Public School, Akron, IA
1924-25	3rd	Sleepy Hollow Public School, Merrill, IA
1925-27	4th & 5th	Merrill Public School, Merrill, IA
Spring 1927	5th	St. Joseph Catholic School,
1927-29	5th & 6th	Le Mars, IA (repeated 5th grade)
Fall 1929	7th	
Spring 1929 thru 33	7th thru 10th	Le Mars Public School, Lemars, IA
1933-34	11th	Herbster Public School, Herbster, WI
1934-35	12th	Port Wing Public School, Port Wing, WI

Upon high school graduation, the Principal and my teachers at Port Wing encouraged me to go on to college and I took their advice. In the fall of 1935, I enrolled as a student at Superior State Teachers College (now known as the University of Wisconsin at Superior), and attended college there until my graduation in June, 1940.

During the summer after I graduated from high school, in 1935, dad got a job as manager and handyman for a large apartment complex in Superior, Wisconsin, the benefits included an apartment for the family. Once again, we sold all the farm machinery and equipment. We packed all of our personal possessions, furniture, hand tools and small garden tools into one large moving van (truck) and moved to Superior in mid-August. Luckily for me and my siblings who were still in school, the apartment was within walking distance of the schools. My college campus was only about one mile from the apartment.

The following spring, 1936, dad found a full time job, bought a house, and we moved from the apartment to our new home at 2608 East 7th (East End), Superior, Wisconsin. Although the new house was still within walking distance of the schools for all of us, it was about three miles from my college campus. Since I had no transportation, I would regularly walk or hitchhike to college, except on those rare days when I could afford a dime for bus fare. Indeed, the Great Depression still had the nation in its grip.

I worked my way through college over the five years I attended (1935-40). During my first three years, I paid my expenses by doing a variety of part time jobs, including washing dishes in the most popular restaurant in the city, assistant mechanic and handyman in the Police Department Garage, and usher in a movie theater. The school time jobs were typically four to eight hours daily, mostly night shifts, and usually five days a week, with a take-home pay of about ten dollars. Additionally, I received $25.00 monthly as a lab assistant in the college chemistry lab, subsidized by a Federal program under the National Youth Administration (NYA). The program was established by President Roosevelt to provide aid for college students from low income families.

During my sophomore year in college, I became a member of the Phi chapter of the Delta Theta fraternity. What fun we had at the regular monthly meetings and social events! The biannual informal dances were great fun, but there was nothing like the annual Frat Formal Ball, at the swankiest ballroom in town, with a popular live dance band. The members of the fraternity, dressed in tuxedos, escorted the prettiest gals in college to the ball. Our dates were all dressed in their fanciest formal gowns. Oh yes, what fond memories linger in my mind.

During my last three years of college, I managed to find time to be actively involved with the Boy Scouts of America. I was an assistant Boy Scout Master and spent a short time as the Scout Master for Troop 20, at St. Francis Xavier Church, East End, Superior. I enjoyed the troop meetings, classes and ceremonies. Additionally, it was a great learning experience, especially being part of the management staff at summer scout camp and jamborees.

I was a member of the college golf team throughout my college years. However, the only golf clubs that I had ever owned were destroyed in our house fire in 1934. Again, I was back to borrowing other people's clubs each time I played. Even with the borrowed clubs, I was usually the low scorer on the team. During my third year of college, while on a routine practice game, I made a hole-in-one. A few days later, I barely missed another hole-in-one on the same hole--only a blade of grass kept the ball from falling in the hole.

In my fourth year of college, I landed a full time job as "Hotel Houseman" at the popular Androy Hotel at 1213 Tower Avenue in downtown Superior. The hotel was built in 1925 and is still in operation today. When it was new, it was known as the city's million dollar hotel, deriving its name from a combination of the names of its original hotel managers, Andrew Doran and Roy Quigley. Each summer I washed all the windows, inside and out, on all of the hotel's eight floors. Whenever any of the high fashion ladies' dogs pooped, guess who was called!

All in all, it was a pretty good job, it paid a whopping $44.00 per month, plus all I could eat at one meal in the hotel restaurant kitchen. The work schedule for summer and vacation time was eight hours a day, six days a week. During the school year I worked four or more hours a day, five days a week. That job paid for all essential expenses for college, and of course, my hair clippers earned a few extra welcome dollars. Semester fees were $19.00 tuition, $10.00 in laboratory fees and about $2.00 or $3.00 for each text book. Everything is relative to its time.

Those college years took their toll. Most of the time, I worked shifts from 5:30 p.m.. to 11:00 p.m., arriving home (by bus after work) about midnight. On weekdays during the school year, I would arise about 6:00 a.m. and arrive at college in time for an 8:00 A.M. class. My last class each day ended at 4:45 p.m. The free hotel-furnished meal at my job was literally a life saver. I weighed 148 pounds on my college entrance physical in August, 1935. After five years of college, on my army enlistment physical exam, I weighed in at 134 pounds.

College Graduation, 1940

Other than the military, finding employment after college graduation was harder than trying to find a needle in a haystack. The military offered room and board, clothing for all seasons, full medical coverage, fifteen days vacation yearly, plus $21.00 per month for the entry rank of Private in the Army. The recruiting Sergeant made the offer sound really too good to pass up-- so-- I decided to enlist.

Overall, my growing up years had been enjoyable, although I was sometimes frustrated by our moving so often. Struggling to survive in hard times, my parents took extraordinary risks in moving from farm to city job or vice versa, in a sort of feast or famine existence. Looking back now, I can better understand their own frustration, in the face of adversity, as well as their resolve to improve their situation.

I know that the turmoil and hardships, that our family

experienced, forged my strong determination to obtain a good education. Very few of my contemporaries went on to college. Indeed, many of my friends dropped out of high school. Some of the few who did enter college soon quit to accept menial jobs, in what appeared to me to be a diminishing job market. Although life was difficult as I worked my way through college, I was determined to graduate.

It seems that my family had been forever on the move. Finally, mom and dad owned their own home. Dad had relatively dependable work doing house remodeling and new construction for a local contractor. I stayed at my parents' home through my five years of college years and, as was typical in those days, I gave my parents as much of my income as I could spare. Those kids who stayed home after high school, whether in college or working, also shared the household expenses.

PART 4

WORLD WAR II
CITIZEN SOLDIERS

IN THE ARMY NOW!

WHILE I WAS IN COLLEGE in the late 1930's, Adolph Hitler was on a rampage of massive aggression and conquest in Europe. America's involvement in that war seemed imminent and all across America, the U.S. military forces initiated special recruiting programs, appealing for volunteers. In June, 1939, my older brother Norbert and younger brother Cyril both responded to the call by enlisting in the National Guard in Superior Wisconsin. Norbert, a master chef, was assigned duty as Mess Sergeant for the Battery Headquarters Company Mess Hall. Cyril was assigned to the same mess hall as an assistant cook. A few months after they enlisted, WWII began in Europe, with Hitler's invasion of Poland on September 1, 1939.

A few days after college graduation, on June 30, 1940, I enlisted as a Private and joined my brothers at the Headquarters Battery (Hq. Btry.), 120th Field Artillery Regiment, 32nd Infantry Division (Red Arrow Division)

Wisconsin National Guard at Superior, Wisconsin. I was assigned to duty as assistant cook in the company mess with my brothers, and with that, we three brothers worked together as cooks for the Hq. Btry. Company mess hall. Thus, as a private and an Army cook, I began my military service.

1941, three military Trautt brothers.
left to right: Norbert, Cyril, me.

Photo taken at Camp Beauregard, Alexandria, Louisiana,
Hq. Battery, 120th Field Artillery Regiment,
32nd Infantry (Red Arrow) Division, Wisconsin Army National Guard.

A month after my enlistment, my rank was upgraded to Private First Class (Pfc.). By mid-August, we had assembled at Camp McCoy, for three weeks encampment and training exercises, and 2 months later, on October 15, 1940, the Wisconsin National Guard was ordered to active Federal service in the U.S. Army.

In early November, 1940, the Superior Wisconsin National Guard units departed Superior by truck convoy, and joined up with the other Wisconsin Guard units at Camp Douglas in Southern Wisconsin. A few days later, the entire 32nd Infantry division proceeded on a seven day military convoy trip to Camp Beauregard, Alexandria, Louisiana. I still have calluses from sitting on the oak bench seats in those canvas covered 2.5 ton military cargo trucks. Upon arrival at Camp Beauregard, we set up camp.

After six months at Camp Beauregard, the Division was relocated to Camp Livingston, Louisiana, only a few miles away. Soon after arriving at Livingston in April, 1941, I requested and received approval for reassignment to telephone operator/lineman. My rank was still Pfc., but, I no longer received the $15/month cook's incentive pay. On October 25, 1941, I reenlisted for three years as a private in the U.S. Army Air Corps (USAAC) and was transferred to Keesler Field, Biloxi, Mississippi to attend Airplane Mechanics School (A.M. School). Again, I started at the bottom, as a Private.

On Sunday, December 7, 1941, Japan attacked Pearl Harbor. I was on a weekend pass to New Orleans, Louisiana and heard the announcement over a storefront radio as I walked down Canal Street. After that announcement came a message from the War Department, "All military personnel report immediately to your military units." I went directly to the bus station and took the first bus back to Keesler Field, arriving in time for a late supper. Reporting to duty, the following morning, December 8, 1941, we received the news that President Roosevelt declared war on Japan.

TRAUTT FAMILY VOLUNTEERS

OF MY PARENTS' TEN CHILDREN who survived to adulthood, six served in the military during World War II and/or the Korean War. Our youngest sibling, Joseph, was too young to enlist during World War II, but served in the Korean War. The service period for each of my siblings is summarized below in order of enlistment date.

Norbert W. Trautt

My older brother Norbert enlisted in the Wisconsin Army National Guard at Superior in June, 1939. He served in the South Pacific for almost four years. At the end of WWII, he returned to the U.S.A. and reenlisted in the Army Air Force. After more than 20 years of service, he was discharged with the rank of Technical Sergeant. He then entered the private sector of the food service industry where he remained until he retired at the age of 65. Norbert married Angela Repose, who had one son by a previous marriage. They had no other children.

Cyril L. Trautt

My younger brother Cyril also enlisted with Norbert in the Wisconsin Army National Guard in June, 1939. He advanced to the rank of Sergeant. He married Marie Bordelon of New Orleans in October, 1941, a month later he requested and was granted a discharge from the army. After leaving the military, Cyril enrolled in Loyola University in New Orleans where he earned a degree in Business Administration. Shortly after his college graduation, he became a Certified Public Accountant and established his own accounting firm in New Orleans. They had no children.

Catherine E. Trautt

My younger sister Catherine enlisted in the Women's Auxiliary Volunteer Emergency Service (WAVES) in Superior, Wisconsin in May, 1943. She completed basic training at Hunters College, New York. She was then transferred to the Naval Air Station, Ottumwa, Iowa, where she attended Cooks and Bakers School. Upon completion of the course, she was assigned to duty as cook at the Air Station and served in that capacity until discharged in October, 1945.

After Catherine was discharged from the military, she

remained in food service and held jobs cooking for Mississippi River boats for several years. She married a U.S. Navy sailor, Charles F. Holt. They had five children: James, Gerald, Rita, Donald and Stephen.

John G. Trautt

My brother John enlisted in the Army on January 25, 1945, at Superior, Wisconsin.

He completed basic training at Fort Riley, Kansas, after which he was transferred to Camp Crowder, Neosho, Missouri, where he attended a course in International Morse Radio Code and Japanese Morse Code. Upon completion of the courses, he was transferred to Vint Hill Farms, Warrenton, Virginia and assigned duty as a monitor of messages transmitted around the world, especially Japanese, German and Russian governmental messages. A few months later he was reassigned as an instructor of three Morse Code tape reading classes of about 40 students each.

On August 4, 1946, after the end of WWII, John requested and received a discharge from the Army. He returned home to his family and job in Superior, Wisconsin. John was employed by the Superior State Bank which was converted to a National Bank in 1948 and renamed Superior National Bank. John married Jessie Sheasby and they had three children, John, Gregory and Deborah. He retired as the bank's vice-president at the age of 65, but he continued serving as active secretary to the executive bank board.

Stephen A. Trautt

Stephen enlisted in the Navy in May, 1944, at 17 ½ years of age (with the permission of our parents). He was the youngest of my siblings to serve in World War II. He served in the South Pacific and was discharged in June, 1946, with the rank of Petty Officer, First Class Boatswain's Mate.

Steven reenlisted in the USAF in August, 1949, and served in the Korean War. In December, 1952, he was discharged from the USAF, with the rank of Staff Sergeant, to accept a GS-3 civil service position in Personnel Management at Scott AFB, Mascoutah, Illinois. He retired at that Base in 1978 with a GS-9 rating (equivalent to the rank of Major).

Stephen married Lucille Riess. They had three children, Anne, Mary and Stephen.

Joseph P. Trautt

Joseph, my youngest sibling, was too young to serve in World War II. However, upon his 18th birthday, in February, 1947, he enlisted in the U.S. Naval Submarine Service, Naval Reserve. Two years later, in July, 1949, he was discharged to reenlist in the USAF.

In the USAF, Joseph served as a military photographer, which included duty as a combat aerial photographer in the Korean War in 1951. The following year, in December, 1952, Joseph was discharged as a Staff Sergeant.

Joseph married Natalie Perebaskine, Ludmila's sister, on November 21, 1953, and then moved to Sacramento, California, where he attended college (Sacramento State College) under the Veteran's (GI Bill) program. Joseph and Natalie had five children: Joseph, Catherine, Lydia, Mary and Michael.

ARMY AIR CORPS
Officer Candidate School

IN JANUARY, 1942, while attending Airplane Mechanics School at Keesler Field, I applied for Army Air Corps Officer Candidate School (OCS). On February 7, 1942, at about 4:00 P.M., I was paged and informed that I was selected to attend OCS, Miami Beach, Florida. Verbal orders were--go eat supper, get packed, and report to Base Headquarters by 6:00 P.M. to board a bus which would take the OCS candidates to the train station in Biloxi, Mississippi.

Wow, what a day, the wind blew, and the dust flew! Finally, on February 7, 1942, at about 7:00 P.M., the train (with sleeper cars) left the station for Miami Beach, Florida. Anyone in grade of Private was promoted to Corporal (Cpl.)when selected for OCS. Not only was I off to OCS, but was now a Corporal! At midterm of OCS, in March, 1942, I was promoted to Staff Sergeant, this promotion was also standard procedure.

A number of famous Hollywood stars and celebrities attended OCS during WWII, including Jimmy Stewart and Clark Gable. In fact, midway through my own OCS period, Clark Gable was one of the new students who arrived for the next class (every six weeks a new class started). Clark Gable, was a handsome Hollywood superstar. Though he was not in any of my classes, we frequently met in the dining hall and at free time events. He was a regular guy and a typical OCS student, congenial and diligently studying and abiding by the rules, hoping, like the rest of us, to become a commissioned officer (2nd Lt.) in the Army Air Forces. Most classes had a failure rate of about 15%, but Clark Gable and I were not among them.   When the war ended, Clark returned to Hollywood to resume his very successful movie career.

Official Photo: 2nd Lieutenant,
U.S. Army Air Forces, OCS Graduation

During the time that I was attending OCS, the Army Air Corps was changed to Army Air Forces. I completed OCS on May 10, 1942. At graduation ceremonies the following day, I was appointed (along with almost 500 graduates) a Commissioned Officer, with the rank of 2nd Lieutenant in the Army of the United States, Army Air Forces (AUS-AAF). I was also issued orders to report to Chanute Field, Rantoul, Illinois, for further training in military administration and personnel management.

A COMMISSIONED OFFICER!
Army Air Forces

ON FEBRUARY 7, 1942, I was off to Officer Candidate School (OCS), Miami Beach, Florida. On May 10, 1942, I graduated from OCS. At graduation ceremonies the next day, along with about 500 graduates, I was appointed a commissioned officer, with the rank of 2nd Lieutenant, US Army Air Forces. The following day, I departed by train for Chanute Field (Rantoul), Illinois. By late afternoon the following day, after an all night train ride, I arrived at Chanute Field and reported to Base Personnel. I was assigned to the 36th Technical School Squadron for four weeks of on-the-job training (OJT) in Staff Administration and Personnel Management. Upon completion of the OJT in mid-June, 1942, I was reassigned to Hq. Army Air Force Technical Training School at Lincoln Field, Nebraska. Two days later, I reported to Lincoln Field and was assigned to duty as Squadron Adjutant (Sq. Adj.).

I was thoroughly enjoying my new assignment when it was abruptly interrupted. After only two weeks as a Sq. Adj., on July 7, 1942, I received new orders from the personnel officer. He informed me that, due to an emergency shortage of Mess Officers and my previous army cook experience, I had been reassigned to the Base Consolidated Mess Squadron. I pleaded to remain in my present assignment, but to no avail. My new duty assignment was mess officer in charge of two 5,000 serving capacity mess halls. What an experience–from a six-month cooking job in the National Guard for 350 soldiers, to Officer-in-Charge of two mess halls serving almost 10,000 soldiers!

In August, 1942, on my own initiative, I organized a sort of "hands-on" Food Service Training program for the monthly arrival of about thirty-five newly assigned cooks' helpers. The program schedule included five phases of on-the-job training.

FIRST THREE DAYS, OBSERVING: The trainees would spend three days just observing all mess hall functions such as cooking, baking and meal preparation.

NEXT FIVE DAYS, HANDS ON: The trainees would spend five days actually assisting the trained food service cooks with a hands-on participation in the actual cooking and baking processes.

OBSERVATIONS: We held a question/discussion session of two hours for the trainees to share their experience and observations.

ASSIGNMENT AS TRAINEES: Trainees were assigned as assistants to a fully trained cook, baker, or butcher for a three-week, one-on-one, hands-on training experience.

PERMANENT ASSIGNMENTS: In this final stage, we assessed the trainees and determined who had performed satisfactorily for the trades and were assigned permanent duty as either a cook, baker, or butcher.

One day during the observation phase of a training session, the Food Service Squadron Commander (a Major) stopped in to observe the proceedings. After the session ended, he asked me to come by his office later in the day. During that office visit, he reminded me about the time, only a few weeks before, when he mentioned that a good soldier performs his assigned duty to the best of his ability even though he might prefer a different assignment. He commented that he was well pleased with my attitude and job performance. He said the main reason he asked me to his office was to find out more about the on-the-job cooking program I had initiated. I can still visualize the major looking me straight in the eye and saying, "Lieutenant, in the military whenever you accomplish something on your own initiative, one of three things may result--nothing, you'll get your butt kicked, or you'll be considered for a staff or command assignment."

Then, again sternly looking at me, he said, "Lieutenant, I'm relieving you of your mess hall duties (my heart stopped beating momentarily) and I am reassigning you as officer-in-charge of a food service training school. You have the organizational and management abilities necessary for this assignment. Now, prepare a curriculum for a Food Service Training School. Also, prepare an itemized list of the equipment, space, personnel and supplies required to equip the school. We will need facilities to train about 30-50 new arrivals of food service personnel each month."

I accomplished the assigned tasks, first with a training school for cooks, a few weeks later with a bakery class, and finally a meat processing class.

The Major in command of the Mess Squadron evidently was pleased with my work, because, on March 22, 1943, I was promoted to First Lieutenant, U.S. Army Air Forces and issued a jeep for my new assignment.

After promotion to 1st Lieutenant, I was issued my first jeep.

AIRPLANE CRASH

IN JULY, 1943, while stationed at Lincoln Air Field, Nebraska, I survived a near-fatal crash in a Piper Cub, two seater, trainer aircraft (designed for a student pilot in the front seat and a flight instructor in the dual control rear seat). On that flight (my very first airplane ride) I was in the rear seat. The purpose of the flight was to locate a site for a field kitchen in the wooded area where several groups of student airplane mechanics were being trained for field operations duties overseas.

As we flew over the training area, the pilot decided to perform a few acrobatics for the troops on the ground below. On his final maneuver, he made a sky dive toward one of the training sites. He failed to pull up in time and plunged into the ground.

As luck would have it, we crashed only about 20 yards from an aircraft maintenance training crew. Personnel at the site rushed to the crashed aircraft and pulled both of us, unconscious, from the wreckage, only moments before the plane exploded and burned.

The pilot suffered an almost severed foot, at the ankle and also sustained multiple lesser injuries. His foot, along with a new stainless steel ankle bone, was successfully reattached. The operation took about five hours and he was hospitalized for almost three months.

I suffered a fractured nose that was flattened and pushed to the right side of my face. That was minor compared to my crushed vertebrae, two in my neck and three in my lower spine. Also, the blow to my head caused a concussion and unconsciousness for about 30 hours. When I awoke, the nurse held a mirror for me to see myself. My entire face was black and blue. I had a metal crown on my head, a metal frame over my shoulders to prevent any movement of my head, and two metal prongs in my nostrils to slowly straighten my nose back to its original position.

Though awake for only a few minutes and hurting from the top of my head to the bottom of my feet, who should appear on the scene but the hospital psychiatrist, a captain and a real nut. He paraded around the room, back and forth, constantly staring at me. He finally approached my bedside and blurted out, "If I put an apple and a thousand-dollar bill on your table here, which would you take?" I vividly recall snapping right back at him that I was hurting enough without his stupid trick, and for him to take his apple and bill and get his G.D. butt the hell out of my room!

Being a college type (book answer theory), he came right back with how I could be court-martialed for what I had just said to a superior officer. I had enough, I hollered, "You're as full of stuffing as a Christmas turkey--now, get your butt out of here!"

With that response he was really getting hot under the collar, and he said that he was going to report me to the Hospital Commander. He did and in only a few moments he returned with the Hospital Commander, a Lt. Colonel. The Commander, who was an M.D., said to the psychiatrist, "What seems to be the problem?" He then repeated what I had said. The Commander looked at me and said, "Lieutenant, at present, I guess you don't really care much for apples or money, do you?" I replied, "No, with all this pain, absolutely not!"

The Commander looked at the psychiatrist and said, "You wanted to know if there was any brain damage. Well you found out, didn't you? I agree with the Lieutenant (me), now leave him alone and let him recuperate!"

After being hospitalized for almost a month, I was released on a 30-day rest and recuperation leave. On a follow-up examination after returning from leave, the doctor explained to me the seriousness of my injuries. He also told me that the long-term effect would be osteo-arthritis of the spine, which would become clearly evident within about 10 to 15 years. He was right. My physical exams for military retirement indicated osteo-arthritic degenerative discs in my neck and lower spine with minimal disability at that time.

PART 5

CHINA-BURMA-INDIA
ASSIGNMENT

INDIA ASSIGNMENT

IN EARLY DECEMBER, 1943, I volunteered for overseas duty (hoping to get an overseas assignment as a Staff Supply Officer or Administrative Officer). A few days later, I received orders to report to Headquarters(Hq.) Caribbean Wing, Air Transport Command (ATC), Miami, Florida, not later than December 27, 1943 for assignment to Hq. India-China (ICWATC), Calcutta, India. En route from Nebraska to Florida, I visited my folks in Superior, Wisconsin.

December 31, 1943, I departed by air for India. Four days later, I arrived at Karachi, India. The flight, by C-54 four engine military passenger aircraft, took us from Florida to India via Puerto Rico, Belem, Brazil, mid-Atlantic ocean Ascension Island, Liberia, West Africa, Algiers, North Africa, Oman, a sultanate located in Southeast Arabia, and then on to Karachi, India. We had made overnight tops at Belem, Ascension Island and Algiers. The very next day after I arrived in India, news was received that the airplane which transported me and 54 other persons had crashed on landing at its next refueling stop. None of the crew or 55 persons on that return flight to the U.S.A. survived the crash.

At the stopover in Algiers, I had spent the evening at the base officers club. Shortly after I was seated, a nicely dressed, young civilian joined me at the bar. I introduced myself and he said, "Pleased to meet you, I'm Nelson Eddy." I replied, "I thought you looked familiar, you must be the Hollywood singer." To which he replied, "Yes, I am." After some pleasantries about our destinations, I asked if he would mind singing a couple of songs for the crowd. For the next hour or so, we talked, ate dinner, and he sang special requested songs. He was part of a USO entertainment group touring US Military installations abroad.

At Karachi, I was assigned to a four week orientation-training class designed to prepare Americans for assignment in India. On February 5, 1944, I departed for Hq. India China Division ICD-ATC, Calcutta, India, for duty assignment. I was issued orders to report to Army Air Force Base, Assam Province, Tezpur, India.

Upon arrival at Tezpur, I requested duty as an Adjutant or Supply Officer. Big Surprise! "Sorry, there is a critical shortage of Mess Officers." In spite of my objection, I was assigned as Assistant Base Mess Officer, because I had been a cook for six months in the National Guard and a Mess Officer in the Army Air Force for about 18 months.

The officer housing area during WWII
in Tezpur, Assam Province, India,
was located on a former tea plantation (above photo)

My billet quarters, in Tezpur, India,
a straw thatched, wood framed structure, for 6 officers.

On my first day of duty at Tezpur, India, I was directed to inspect all the mess halls on the air base and submit a written report of my findings. Overall, I found the food preparation and serving to be satisfactory. However, some of the mess halls were experiencing serious sanitation problems. The grease separator tanks for kitchen waste water were frequently clogging up and overflowing onto the ground causing a stinking mud hole just outside of the kitchens. There was no doubt about it, the 20 gallon grease separator tanks were much too small to handle the large volume of greasy kitchen waste water that was being generated and processed through the system daily.

A couple of days later, I searched the base salvage yard and found some 55 gallon oil drums. I calculated they were about the right size for the system I wanted to configure to correct the kitchen waste water grease problem. After obtaining authorization, I proceeded to design and construct a prototype grease separator system using the two 55 gallon oil drums connected in tandem, providing total volume of about 100 gallons for the system. I installed the tanks at one of the mess halls and then observed the system in operation for a few days.

These tanks were installed in the ground and were connected to plumbing from the kitchen sinks.

Clean-out Lid   Clean-out Lid

Greasy kitchen water IN   Grease floats to top   Residue grease floats to top   Greaseless water OUT to leach lines

Water from the draining kitchen sinks flowed through the system.

Photo of our grease separator tanks fabricated from base salvage.

Eureka! My oil drum contraption functioned perfectly. My request to install the separator tanks at all base mess halls was speedily approved. Finally, after about a month, all the mess halls were equipped with the system and my project was satisfactorily completed. Years later, in 1969, after working a short time for the Yolo County Health Department, Woodland, California, I realized that I had unknowingly reinvented the Imhof sewage disposal septic tank system with my grease separator system.

On March 4, 1944, the Base Mess Officer was transferred to another Air Base. Then, I was reassigned as Base Mess Officer in charge of seven troop mess halls and one Officers' club and mess hall. Only a few days after assuming my new duties, an unusual population explosion of house flies swarmed over the base. Never had I seen so many flies. They became a real nuisance, especially around the mess halls and dining rooms. Some insecticides were sprayed on the base in areas away from troop concentrations. However, chemical spraying was not feasible around the mess halls because of the proximity to food being prepared and served.

I studied the situation and observed the behavior of the flies at length. I noted that the house flies tended to jump upward and forward on takeoff and reasoned that some kind of a cone shaped screen trap with bait underneath might succeed in trapping them by forcing them up into a screened holding container. I was willing to try any safe, non-chemical method of controlling the fly population near the mess halls, especially in the kitchens and dining rooms.

So again, it was back to the drawing board. That night, after the troops (and flies) settled in for the night, I designed and constructed a prototype fly trap. The following morning, I placed the trap next to a garbage rack near one of the mess halls where the flies swarmed in a feasting frenzy. I guess it is common knowledge that flies seem to like most of the foods which humans eat, especially if it has an aroma of decay. I placed a piece of yesterday's meat bones underneath the fly trap and then waited. Lo and behold, the noxious little vermin swarmed to the meat bone, dined, hopped forward and flew upward, landed inside the cone and walked upward through the small hole at the top into a screened holding area.

The following day, I invited Col. Gowins, the Base Commander, and several other officers and sergeants, to observe my non-chemical, environmentally safe insect trap in action. Col. Gowins was impressed and ordered the Base Installation's Shop Officer (also present) to construct fly traps for all the mess halls, latrines, and any other locations where flies were a nuisance.

Incidentally, a few days after the traps were in use, some of the indigenous employees (having no aversion to flies but with a religious belief in the sanctity of all life) were observed opening the traps and letting the live flies escape. Next, I installed locks on the traps--no more escapees.

functional fly-traps

I don't know if anyone made a similar fly trap before I made mine in Tezpur, India, in 1944. However, about 25 years later, while working for the Yolo County Health Department, while inspecting food production facilities and farms, I came across insect traps of all kinds, shapes and sizes purchased from hardware and farm supply stores.

One day during the hot Indian jungle summer of 1944, I had a brainstorm to construct an ice maker. While sorting out items at the base salvage junk yard, for use in the mess halls, I found a wrecked jeep with an undamaged motor. Near the jeep was a pile of used and damaged high pressure tubing and valves, metal tanks and all kinds of scrap metal. In my mind (remembering the chapter on the principle of refrigeration in my college physics class) I could visualize everything needed to construct an ice making machine--and it was all there in that pile of junk!

The next task was to find (among the troops) anyone willing to help sort through the junk and remove the jeep motor. Within a few days, I found a refrigeration engineer (with a B.S. Degree), an automotive mechanic, and a couple of experienced refrigeration repair men. One evening, the five of us went to the salvage yard. We retrieved the jeep motor and a small truck load of tubing, tanks, valves, and electrical wiring. The next evening the refrigeration engineer and I made drawings of an ice maker.

The following day, spurred on by the hot jungle climate, we began the assembly of the ice maker. Each day the weather seemed to be hotter. The thought of ice at the end of the tunnel kept us working harder and longer each evening after the end of the regular workday. In less than a month of very hard and tedious work and many banged-up fingers, a real honest-to-goodness jungle monster contraption ice maker materialized. Finally, we were ready for a test run. We started the machine and in amazement observed the formation of ice crystals in the freezer tanks. In less than an hour, that odd-looking monstrosity produced a 25 lb. block of ice.

Anticipating a successful production of ice, I had previously borrowed a one gallon hand-operated ice cream maker from a local merchant in Tezpur. That evening the temperature was about 100°F and just looking at that ice forming was great. I suggested to the crew that we invite Col. Harry W. Gowins, the Base Commander, to our celebration and that he be our taste tester for our first batch of special jungle ice cream.

About 10:00 P.M. the ice cream was being processed. I phoned the commander at his quarters and asked, "Would you like a nice big dish of real cold ice cream before retiring for the evening?" His reply, "Damn it, Ed, it's just too hot and miserable to be joking!" I replied that it was no joke and that the ice cream would be ready in about the time it would take for him to walk to the Food Service warehouse. He evidently didn't think it was a joke, since he appeared on the scene just as we were preparing to serve it. Upon entry, he commented, "Ed, where in the Hell did you steal the ice to make ice cream?"

"Well, Colonel," I said, "just look over there. That monster of a contraption is an ice maker, made from junk from our salvage yard, and this is the crew that helped construct it." Of course, the Colonel was first to be served and then the rest of us in the military pecking order.

Now that I had reliable supply of ice, I requisitioned a five gallon electric powered ice cream maker from the Army Supply Depot in Calcutta, and within a matter of days, ice cream was served to the troops in one mess hall to the surprise and amazement of all. After that, each mess hall was served ice cream once a week. We were the only Army Air Force Base in the Indian jungle serving ice cream and iced beverages that summer of 1944.

OVERLY EAGER INSPECTOR

IT SEEMED that the Base Administrative Inspector, a captain, whose responsibility it was to keep the Base Commander apprized of the current status of all base functions, was a bit envious of the high ratings my unit received from the Hq. ATC inspectors. He was diligently watching my unit, trying to catch us doing something wrong or failing to comply with regulations, like a game of "gotcha". Whenever he had an opportunity, at the Officer's Club or at routine base meetings, he would sarcastically refer to my unit as "Ed's Gourmet Greasy Spoon." All my life I've had a zero tolerance for rude and sarcastic persons.

I guess it was bound to happen sooner or later. One day, while inspecting the mess halls, the inspector thought he had finally caught my unit in violation of a food service storage regulation. He found beetles in a mess hall rice storage bin. He told the Mess Sergeant that he was going to the Base Commander's office to report what he had found. The Mess Sergeant, almost in panic, phoned the information to me. I instructed him to gather up all the sifters he could find and immediately put all available troops to work sifting the beetles from the rice and that I'd get to the mess hall posthaste. I arrived at the mess hall just as the troops finished the sifting. About two or three minutes later, the inspector arrived with the Base Commander.

Upon arrival, the Commander said, "I've been informed that the bulk grain foods are contaminated with beetles." "Gosh," I replied, "that's news to me and I'd like the Captain to show me just where he found the beetles." The inspector proceeded to the rice bin and scooped up some rice, and proclaimed, "Colonel, the beetles are right here in this bin." What! No beetles in that first scoop, so, he scooped deeper. Still, no beetles. Going still deeper in the bin, red-faced, sweating, and mumbling to himself, "I know they're in here because I found some only a few moments ago."

Finally, the Colonel said jokingly, "Well, Captain, maybe you scared them enough on your first visit that they all flew away." At that the Commander departed for his office, leaving the inspector standing there, still red-faced, sweating profusely and blubbering gibberish about me having done something to the rice or replaced it with another bin of good rice. I asked him, "How could I? I arrived at the mess hall only seconds before you and the Commander."

The "gotcha" score this time was in my favor. Of course, the following day, I inspected all of the rice and grain foods for grain beetles. Any found to be contaminated with beetles were disposed of in accordance with regulations. We contracted with local farmers who would pick up such food items and leftovers from the mess hall for animal feed.

That inspector was one determined little bugger. The following week he made another surprise inspection of the mess halls, hoping he would find some discrepancy that he could report to the Base Commander and possibly redeem himself.

Unable to find any infraction of regulations that were serious enough to report, he noticed some cook's helpers and the Kitchen Police (KP) cleanup crew not wearing upper garments. He ordered them to put on T-shirts or some other cook's upper garment. The troops told him that they had permission from their commander (me) to do non-cooking jobs without upper garments on extremely hot days. He asked for the Mess Sergeant, who in turn also stated that only persons preparing or serving food were required by regulations to wear upper garments. The Captain then ordered anyone "without upper garments" to immediately put one on, they all complied. Another "got ya", he thought.

After the Captain left, the Mess Sergeant phoned me and told me what had happened. I immediately phoned the Base Commander and reported the incident. He asked me to come to his office for a conference with him and the inspector. At the meeting, I again explained what the Mess Sergeant reported to me.

The inspector admitted that he conducted a surprise inspection, without me or my authorized representatives being present. He also admitted that he ordered the KP's to put on upper garments even after the Sergeant told him that they had my permission to work without upper garments on extremely hot days.

The Base Commander then told the inspector it seemed, from recent inspection reports, that the inspector was not adequately informed regarding regulations pertinent to operational compliance. Next came a lecture on "Protocol" quoting directly from the Army Inspector's Manual. Simply put, out of common decency and military courtesy, the inspector should ask to be accompanied by the unit commander or his authorized representative. Chalk up a "gotcha" for me.

I seldom saw the inspector after that very informative conference. However, each time he made an inspection of my unit after that, he politely requested me or one of my officers to accompany him on the inspection tour and always rendered a written report of his observations.

In October, 1944, the annual Hq. ICD-ATC Operational Readiness Inspection (ORI) of our base was made. My base mess-supply unit received an outstanding rating with special mention of all the homemade equipment that I had manufactured for the mess halls from salvaged military equipment and materials, including the grease separators, ice maker and fly traps, as well as other items, such as oil burning hot water heaters made from 55 gallon oil drums, work benches, utility sinks, etc. Shortly afterwards, on November 1, 1944, I was promoted to Captain and reassigned to Hq. ICD-ATC, Calcutta. My one-year assignment at Tezpur Army Air Force Base in the Assam Valley jungle of India had been a markedly memorable learning and maturing experience for me.

A STRICT BUT FAIR COMMANDER

OVER THE YEARS, I was often asked by my children if, during the war, I had been rough and mean like so many characters portrayed in war movies. In retrospect, I recall that from the time I received my commission in the Army Air Forces and for the tenure of my military service, I had the reputation of being strict but fair with my subordinates.

One example, which I believe illustrates the manner in which I supervised and/or commanded my military units, is an episode which took place when I was stationed in Tezpur, India. At that time I was a 1st Lt., assigned to an Army Air Force Base in Tezpur (Assam Province), India. I was Officer-in-Charge of the Base Food Service and Supply unit, consisting of about 250 personnel. Routinely, I scheduled weekly meetings of all personnel, no one exempt except for previously scheduled duty. I emphasized performance of duty, to the best of one's ability and personal good conduct. These being the building blocks or key elements for promotion and future positions of increased responsibility, a sort of "up the proverbial military ladder" to a successful military career. And of course, everyone at the group meetings was encouraged to present job-related problems for discussion and possible solution. This concept eventually became my "modus operandi for the duration of my military career.

After becoming a commissioned officer, it didn't take me very long to realize that daily inspections of the functions under my supervision, were really prime time for me to monitor the progress of each section. It was also prime time for the Officer or NCO in charge of each section to present work-related problems, for a one-on-one discussion and, generally, an on the spot solution.

After a couple of months on an assignment, I became acquainted with all my officers and soldiers and was equally aware of the quality of their job performance. Occasionally, I would conclude the group meeting with a reminder that all who performed their duties to the best of their ability and exhibited good military demeanor, would be recommended for promotion when the next promotion cycle came around. Finally, that day arrived and I forwarded to Headquarters the names of those I believed to be qualified and deserving of promotion. I justified each recommendation with comments about job performance and conduct. The result was that the Headquarters Promotion Board promoted all the personnel that I had rated as outstanding. Our unit had received more promotions (on a percentage basis) than any other Army Air Force unit in India.

To clarify this story, I must interject some explanation. Shortly before the promotion cycle, Hq. ICD-ATC conducted an annual Base Operational Readiness Inspection (ORI). My Tezpur unit was rated overall "Outstanding," the only Air Forces Food Service/Supply unit in India that was rated so highly. However, due to the high number of promotions received by my unit, some ATC Commanders complained to Hq. ATC and challenged the promotions. A Brigadier General was dispatched to investigate those complaints.

In meeting with the General (I was only a 1st Lt.) I presented him with a copy of the recent Hq. ATC ORI report, of which he informed me he was already familiar. After he reviewed it again, he suggested a check of the personnel files and supply records, as first business of the day. After spending considerable time checking the records, he turned to me and said, "I find everything in these records in excellent order." So, it was off to an inspection of the Food Service and Supply functions. When about halfway through the sections, the General turned to me and said, "I think I've seen enough to convince me why your Food Service and Supply unit was indeed rated outstanding. Furthermore, my report will state that all those promoted were exceptionally well qualified, as verified by the annual Headquarters Inspection and all were justifiably rewarded with a well-earned promotion. Case closed."

MOBILE FOOD SERVICE TRAINING TEAM

AS PREVIOUSLY MENTIONED, the Hq. ICD-ATC Operational Readiness Inspection (ORI) of our Tezpur Base was conducted in early October, 1944 and my base Food Service/Supply unit received an outstanding rating. Shortly afterwards, on November 1, 1944, I was promoted to Captain, Army Air Force and three days later I was transferred from Tezpur to Hq. ICD-ATC, Calcutta, India. My new assignment was Officer-in-Charge (OIC) of a "Mobile Food Service/Supply Inspection and Training Team."

Before being transferred from Tezpur to Calcutta, I was directed to select a well-trained group consisting of one Mess Officer and twenty fully qualified food service personnel from my unit, for transfer to a new Army Air Force Base in China. I made the selection and forwarded the names to Hq. ATC. About two weeks later, the group was transferred to China.

After my experience and learning process in dealing with the Base Administrative Inspector at the Tezpur Army Air Force Base, I really believed that I was ready and qualified for the new assignment. That Captain inspector had unknowingly prepared me exceptionally well on the do's and don'ts of conducting an administrative inspection. But, most of all, I never forgot the Base Commander's words of wisdom, when he lectured the Captain, while reading directly from the Inspector's Manual:

(1) remember protocol, common decency, and military courtesy,

(2) always be accompanied by the Unit Commander or his representative on all inspections,

(3) avoid being too negative by not only reporting discrepancies of noncompliance with regulations, but also by reporting on personal or unit performance of excellence, and

(4) provide a copy of the written report to the Unit Commander as well as the Base Commander.

After that unusual learning experience from the Captain's style of inspection and negative reporting, there was no doubt in my mind that I was prepared and ready to begin my new assignment of "Chief of the Food Service Inspection/Training Team," to tour China-Burma-India (CBI) Army Air Force Bases. Did you notice the new name? About that time the Air Force began slowly changing "Mess" to "Food Service."

On November 4, 1944, I arrived at Hq. ICD-ATC, Calcutta. The next day, Col. Earle E. Hamm, Director of Materiel, explained my duties as OIC of the Food Service Inspection Team. A few days later, my team and I departed by air for Kunming, China, to begin our inspections.

That assignment took me and my team of three Sergeants (one Master Sergeant and two Tech. Sergeants) by air travel to all CBI Army Air Force Bases to inspect food service, supply and base exchange facilities and to train food service personnel in the manufacture and use of homemade food service equipment. We visited CBI bases for almost one year inspecting food service and supply functions and constructing hot water heaters, sinks, fly-traps, work tables, storage bins, sewage waste systems, etc., from all kinds of salvaged military equipment and materials.

After completing only two base inspections, Hq. ATC temporarily delayed the inspections and directed me to accompany a Chinese Army Captain (appointed by Chinese Army General Chiang Kai-shek) to make a survey to determine which local foods (such as pork, poultry, vegetables, fruits, and grains) could be procured for the military troops in China.

I was to meet the Captain at the Kunming, China, Army Air Force Base, receive instructions, and then proceed with the

Captain on a one month food survey. The survey plans directed us to travel throughout that portion of China not occupied by the Japanese Army or the Chinese Communist rebels. We had a prearranged plan, in the event that we lost contact, I would try to locate the local town or village elder. The Captain would always, when arriving in a survey area, contact the local elder and give him information about the purpose of the food survey and his whereabouts while in the area. The elder was also a great help in getting the word out to anyone who had produce for sale.

Early one morning, I was scheduled to meet the Captain at an open-air market in the city of Chen Chung (if I remember correctly). Unable to find him at the designated location, I inquired at various market stalls, "Does anyone speak English?" Finally, after several attempts, a young boy, about 12 years old, spoke up, saying, "Yes, I speak English a leetle bit." I asked him if he could direct me to the town elder. His reply was "Yes, follow me, his home is very close on the edge of town." We proceeded by rickshaw to the home of the town elder. Generally, the elder in each village or town, as I came to find out, was a distinguished, well-educated, usually bearded, and friendly older gentleman, who was highly respected and admired in the community. He was also sort of a walking Encyclopedia of local events.

After we arrived at the elder's residence, a small quaint, typically Ming Dynasty style home, the young boy introduced me to the elder in Chinese. I asked, "Do you speak English?" The elder then said, "No, parlez-vous Francais?" My reply was no, then I asked, "Sprechen Sie Deutsch?" A huge smile came over his face and he responded with "Ja, Jawohl!"

There I was, up in the northern interior of China speaking college German to a Chinese elder who also spoke college German, among other languages. That was the first time I put my four years of college German classes to good use. As custom would have it, Chinese tea and cookies were in order. During the conversation, while sipping tea, he explained that he received a Ph.D. in chemistry from the University of Heidelberg, Germany (if I remember correctly). He had been a professor of chemistry at a Chinese university, and had recently retired.

At the conclusion of our tea time, the friendly old gentleman gave me the address of the Hotel where the Captain had registered. The young boy then escorted me, again on foot, alongside the rickshaw, to the hotel which was only a few blocks away. I tipped the young boy and the rickshaw handler generously and we parted. I found the Captain, then we were off again to the village open-air market on the food survey mission.

When one is busy, time seems to fly. We completed the survey in thirty-two days. In early January, 1945, I returned to Hq. ATC in Calcutta, India to deliver my survey report and brief General Tunner, Commander of ATC, and take a few days vacation. The Chinese Captain reported back to Chinese Army Hq., Kunming, China, to deliver his report and to brief General Chiang Kai-shek. Procurement of available produce and other food items, for U.S. Forces in China, was now the responsibility of the Procurement Section at Hq. ATC.

UNDER ENEMY ATTACK

IN MAY 1944, US and allied ground forces under the command of General Joseph Stilwell, captured the Japanese air base at Myitkyina, Burma. Only a few days later, US cargo aircraft began airlifting military equipment over the Himalaya Mountains ("The Hump") into China, for General Chiang Kai-shek.

Only a few days after the airlift operation began, Japanese fighter pilots shot down some of the cargo planes. The US Air Force fighter pilots responded immediately and shot down so many Japanese aircraft, that the Japanese ceased the air attacks.

Then, in late 1944, having failed in their air attack program, the Japanese ground forces decided to retake Myitkyina Air Base. They were within artillery range on the march toward the base.

In mid-January, 1945, after a few days of military leave, I departed Hq. ATC, Calcutta, on a flight to China, via Burma, with a planned en route inspection stopover at the Myitkyina, Burma U.S. Army Air Force Base. I vividly remember the turn of events on that flight. As the pilot was preparing for final approach for landing, just before dusk, he received instructions from the Base Tower to come in low and fast. The Japanese artillery was shelling the base outposts and base perimeter. Their infantry was not far behind ready and poised for an attack on the base.

The pilot followed instructions and as we were approaching the runway, the plane was hit with 20 mm ground fire, suffering minor damage to the aircraft, but no casualties. After landing on the runway, the pilot was directed to taxi to the far end of the base runway--pull into an aircraft bunker--disembark everyone–and hit the ground running like a cheetah for the nearest air raid shelter. We did. Later, we were bused to the mess hall for a nervous supper meal. After supper, we were each issued infantry rifles and then bussed to the billets and ordered to stand by (more nervous waiting). At about 2:30 A.M., the Japanese stopped the artillery shelling, followed by our Army doing likewise. Total silence, no artillery or infantry arms fire could be heard, it was a weird, eerie silence.

The U.S. Army Infantry and base perimeter defenses were entrenched, prepared and waiting for what was thought to be an imminent attack. By daylight, still no arms fire was heard. A search patrol was dispatched to survey the situation. No enemy personnel or military equipment could be sighted. The Japanese, with their dead, guns, and equipment, had slipped away under cover of darkness and retreated into the jungle. A team was dispatched to inspect the battlefield and search for arms and equipment left behind by the Japanese.

The Base Commander permitted me to accompany the search team. Everyone was briefed on safety concerning mines and booby traps, as well as the possibility of sniper fire. Evidently, the Japanese retreated too rapidly to set up such systems. Everyone in the search party found considerable quantities of rifles, bayonets, swords, as well as small tools and equipment. I found a Japanese Infantry rifle, an Indian Gurkha hand-fighting knife and a Japanese mess kit. Regulations required all guns to be turned into supply, however, other items could be retained. I kept the Gurkha knife as part of my WWII memorabilia, and gave it to my son John for his 50th birthday in May, 2005. The Army Defense commander and his war staff were unable to determine why the Japanese suddenly withdrew and disappeared into the hilly jungle. They appeared to be headed east and south toward an ocean port.

With the problem of the attack on the Base being apparently greatly reduced or over, I proceeded with my inspection of the Food Service and Supply functions. After a couple of days we completed the inspection and delivered a report to the Base Commander. The following day, my team of three Sergeants and I flew on to China to conduct more inspections. During our tour of U.S. Air Bases in China, we experienced some Japanese bombing raids. Luckily though, none of my team were injured, mostly just shaken up a bit.

THE TREACHEROUS HIMALAYAS

ONE DAY IN MARCH, 1945, in the mid afternoon, I boarded a two-engine C47 passenger aircraft at Kunming, China, AF Base, with destination (if I remember correctly) Lilliyang, China. After flying for sometime, a non-forecasted cloud cover blanketed the ground below and ahead of us. A short time later, the radio communication equipment aboard the aircraft became inoperable and the cloud cover became more dense. With no communication with our base destination or any other base, the pilot reversed direction 180□ and headed back to Kunming. Incidentally, Kunming is located on a plateau at an elevation of about 5,000 feet above sea level.

The aircraft crew became noticeably tense and the pilot announced that the radio was still out of order and that the ground cover was too dense to see any terrain below. He said that he would continue in the direction of Kunming above the clouds, hoping that he would find clear skies in that area. As time passed, the situation became more tense.

The sun would be setting in about a half hour, still no glimpse of the terrain below, and no communication with any air base. The pilot advised: "Prepare for a crash landing . . . we will continue on course until low on gas, then descend through the clouds at a slow speed, and hope to break out underneath the clouds and find a flat stretch of the plateau to land on."

We flew on for about fifteen more minutes or so, then sort of out of nowhere, about a quarter of a mile directly ahead, a 150 yard diameter opening appeared in the clouds. The pilot let out a war whoop, "Land ho! There's an opening dead ahead and I can see terra firma far enough below the clouds for a safe descent." The pilot quickly descended through the opening, thinking it might soon close up. After descent, he found the bottom of the cloud layer to be about 4000 feet above the terrain below. Maintaining the direction toward Kunming, the pilot soon announced sighting a ground marker indicating we were only a few minutes from the Kunming Air Base.

No crash landing after all, what a wonderful sigh of relief by all aboard! As we taxied up to the terminal, the sun was just setting and disappearing over the horizon. At the terminal, I asked some of the troops what they were thinking about as we descended through the opening in the clouds. It was unanimous, they all quickly replied that they were too busy praying to be thinking about anything else.

To digress a little, while stationed at Tezpur in India, I often listened to pilots at the Officer's Club comparing stories over drinks of frightening experiences on flights over the Himalaya Mountains, "the Hump." Although I very much enjoyed listening to the stories, some of them were hard to believe, such as being caught in blinding rain or snow storms, unbelievably high wind velocities, powerful up and down drafts (known now as wind-shear phenomenon) and having ice form on the leading edges of the aircraft wings and nose on a perfectly clear day. Most of the stories seemed a little like fishermen tales, especially to me, a non-flying, administrative staff officer.

Later, I became a true believer after my own frightening experience on a flight over the Himalayas. As Chief of the Mobile Food Service Inspection team, I made flights to all regions of China, Burma and India. In that one year, I probably accumulated as much or more air time than many of the pilots. Well, one summer afternoon on a flight from India to China, over the Himalaya Mountains, aka "The Hump", I experienced one of those unbelievable phenomenons. From that day to this, I quit doubting the seemingly exaggerated stories told by aircraft pilots.

The flight was in a four-engine C-54 passenger/cargo aircraft. When we took off from India, for what we expected to be a normal flight, the weather was great with clear skies and only light winds. All that quickly and drastically changed once we were over the Himalayas. We were flying along at an altitude of about 31,000 feet, enjoying a nice smooth flight with a clear and beautiful bird's eye view of the snow-capped mountains below. Then I noticed ice forming almost instantly on the leading edge of the wings. The pilot, knowing what was occurring, quickly descended to a level below the mountain tops to a lower and warmer altitude. Soon, the ice was melting and breaking off in chunks which slammed into the fuselage of the plane making sounds as loud as shotgun blasts. As soon as the ice melted, the pilot ascended back above the mountain tops. After only moments, ice again began to form extremely fast on the wings.

Down we went again, but before we had descended low enough for the ice to melt, the plane flew into a horrible updraft that pushed the plane quickly above the mountain tops. At that altitude, the plane continued a rapid buildup of more ice and then flew into an almost disastrous down draft that very rapidly dropped the plane to a dangerously low altitude between the mountain peaks, while simultaneously bouncing the hell out of the plane. The pilot, about scared out of his wits, knowing full well what was happening, circled the smaller mountains, sometimes at almost tree top levels, finally made a bee-line for the valley ahead and safe passage out of the mountains and back to India.

After landing, the pilot taxied directly to the terminal. As we prepared to deplane, I noticed that the pilot and the copilot were both ghostly white and noticeably trembling. The pilot seemed more shaken up than did the copilot. As the co-pilot passed by me on the way off the aircraft, I asked him what had happened. Incidentally, I was the only passenger aboard the aircraft, everything else was cargo for U.S. military bases in China. He explained that aircraft seldom survive what our plane had just passed through.

All I can say now, it was a good thing that I didn't realize the seriousness of the situation or I probably would have turned green instead of white. During the episode in the mountains, I was thinking, my God, what a horribly rough and bumpy flight, as I bounced all over the freight, hanging on for dear life with all my strength.

I found out the next morning that several aircraft and crews were lost that late afternoon and night in the strange and treacherous weather which our pilot had somehow managed to fly safely out of and back to India. That pilot started to become prematurely gray only a short time after that flight and was totally white-haired in just a few months. He developed a total and complete fear of flying and was returned to the States for release and discharge from the service. During the time that I was stationed in India, I knew of one other pilot who suffered a similar fate after flying the Hump for a few months. Some months later, I was told by the attending doctor that he was not sure what caused the premature whitening of the hair. He explained that it could have been psychological or hereditary, or maybe a combination of both.

One day, when having lunch with General Turner and staff, I discussed my experience flying over the Hump between India to China. The trip was about 500 miles across the Hump, flying time in a C-54 passenger aircraft was four to five hours, depending on the weather.

General Turner explained that winds up to 100 miles an hour (sometimes even more) blowing into the steep barren mountain slopes would glance off the slopes to create updrafts over the mountain ridges and down drafts into the valleys below. Planes caught in a down draft could drop at a rate of 5,000 feet per minute, and then suddenly be carried upward at almost the same speed. Also, the turbulence could flip an airplane upside down. Icing on the plane was also a problem above 12,000 feet, sometimes bending or warping the wings from the buildup of ice. I know these to be true because I personally experienced them in flights over the Hump mountain ranges.

NOT A ROUTINE INSPECTION

DURING MY INSPECTION of Army Air Force Bases in China in late April, 1945, I finally arrived at Changtu (or was it Changking?), at the base where my selected group of 21 outstanding food service personnel were stationed. I had actually almost forgotten about the group, but shortly after my arrival at the Base, I found out that the group had definitely not forgotten me.

What a surprise and honor! Four of the topnotch NCO's from my former unit in India met me upon arrival. They transported me to the Administrative Office for the Mess and Supply unit. As we arrived, there stood the Mess Officer, Lt. Fred A. Hayley, my former assistant, the Mess Sergeant, the cooks, and the supply personnel, all lined up in parade formation, ready for a troop inspection. They all looked like they had just stepped out of a tailor shop in brand new uniforms, with the brass and leather shined to a mirror perfection.

Actually, I was surprised, because such an honor of troop inspection is usually reserved for visiting Headquarter's Commanders or their division staff chiefs. I was only a Captain with a team of one Master Sergeant and two Technical Sergeants, on an inspection and training mission to the base. What to do? Well--after graciously accepting the good will gesture--I obliged the Lieutenant and accommodated the group of soldiers with a first class "Inspection of the Troops." That completed, I was then escorted to the Mess Hall where the Mess Officer, the Mess Sergeant and all the cooks stood at attention in a reception line. The cooks, dressed in white uniforms looked like French Chefs prepared to perform an exciting food ritual.

The Mess Officer welcomed me and my team to a special dinner in my honor as their "Past Commander" (as the Lieutenant said), whom they held in high esteem. What a special group of soldiers--unbelievable! I reminded them that I was there to conduct an inspection of their performance in the Food service and Supply functions. Their unanimous reply, "We're ready!"

After two days of intensive observation, I completed the inspection. Again, I was pleasantly surprised, all unit functions were found to be operating in an outstanding manner. The entire unit appeared to be a mirror image of their training and performance when assigned to my unit in Tezpur, India. The Base Commander concurred fully with my inspection report and expressed his belief that he had the best Army Air Forces Food Service-Supply Unit in China.

A short time later, a Hq. ATC, Calcutta Staff Service-Supply Team performed another inspection of the Base, and again, the Food Service unit was rated outstanding in all functions, that inspection confirmed my previous inspection rating. Not long after the inspection, the Hq. ATC Service-Supply Section Chief wrote an article for the weekly Hq. ATC Bulletin, which was distributed to all CBI Air Base Commanders. The article stated that the unit was considered the "number one" Air Forces Food Service-Supply Unit in China. He also included a comment that the unit was previously assigned to and trained by me, Lt. Trautt, at the Tezpur, India, Air Force Base, prior to their assignment to the Base in China and that Lt. Hayley, using some of my design ideas, had also constructed considerable mess hall equipment from discarded salvage yard junk.

During my visit to that base, the Base Commander received a radio message that Berlin fell on May 2, 1945. A few days later, at my next inspection stop, word was received that Nazi Germany surrendered on May 7, 1945, at a school house in

Rheims, Germany. Now, we must turn our efforts into the defeat and surrender of the Japanese.

FOOD SERVICE TRAINING SEMINAR

ALTHOUGH THE WAR in Europe had ended, there was a war still raging in Asia. In mid-May 1945, my team of technicians and I flew to Hq. China Wg. ATC, Kunming, China, to continue Food Service and Supply inspections. While in Kunming, I decided that a training seminar was needed to demonstrate the homemade equipment that I designed and constructed for mess halls when I was stationed at Tezpur, India while attempting to improve the food service for the troops. Brigadier General W.H. Tunner, Commander, Hq. ICD-ATC, Calcutta, India, approved my request to conduct the proposed seminar at the Kunming U.S. Army Air Base. I proceeded to plan for it with three separate demonstrations covering mess hall renovation, mess equipment made from salvaged materials, and creative recipes using mostly dehydrated and/or canned food.

A notice regarding the demonstration seminar was sent to each Commander of the several surrounding U.S. Air Bases. They were encouraged to send to the seminar key Officers and NCO's involved in food service, supply and/or maintenance. The response was exceptional, over fifty personnel were directed to attend the seminar.

The Flight Line Passenger Service Mess Hall was to be used both as the model for the mess hall renovation seminar and as the classroom for the seminar. In preparation for the seminar, I had the sidewalks and parking lot of the mess hall surfaced with gravel. There were two dining rooms in the mess hall building. The far right wing was for officers, and the left wing was for non-commissioned officers and enlisted persons. The kitchen was located in the center and served both dining rooms. The mess hall served four meals daily, breakfast, dinner, supper and a midnight meal.

In the above photo, I am standing with my assistant, Tech. Sgt. "Bud" Borden from California, on the new gravel pathway to the mess hall where the seminar was to take place. Bud supervised the gravel path with border detail and the sign above the mess hall.

The dining room before renovation (above) was a place to eat 3 meals a day, but after renovation (below photo), it also was a place to relax, to eat, and to enjoy the atmosphere. The coverings on the ceiling, windows, and tablecloths were made from discarded air drop chutes which we retrieved from the base salvage yard.

Flight Line Passenger Mess Hall, Kunming, 1945.

Most of the U.S. Air Force base mess halls in China were equipped with open top grate charcoal burning cook stoves without fume exhaust pipes, resulting in smoke filled kitchens. Sinks were too small for U.S. Military cooking pots and pans.

I found the facilities and equipment for the kitchens to be significantly inadequate, while the base salvage yards seem to be filled with an abundant source of usable materials and discarded equipment that could be reused to construct kitchen tools and equipment. The old adage, "necessity is the mother of invention," was never more true for anyone with a little imagination.

There was no plumbing to the kitchen when I arrived, only a hand operated water pump located about 10-feet outside the kitchen. Water was being hand pumped into pails, carried into the kitchen and heated on the stove.

My team of technicians and I were able to make good use of those salvage yards, outfitting our kitchens by fabricating cook stoves, sinks for washing and sterilizing, sinks for washing dishes and tableware, and also by plumbing hot and cold running water to the sinks. Not only did we construct hot and cold running water systems, we also built and installed a sterilizing tank with a combustion chamber underneath the sinks to sterilize mess kits, dishware and tableware. Cleanliness and sanitation practices were a big part of this training program.

To supply running water, we first built a thirty foot tower to hold eight 55 gallon steel oil drums, these provided a gravity flow water supply to the kitchen.

Using 3 oil drums, we constructed a hot water heater with a pressure relief valve, to which we attached a cast iron exhaust pipe (4 inches in diameter) from the combustion chamber at the bottom, up through the center and out the top of the water drums.

After installing the water distribution piping, we were then able to pipe both hot and cold running water to kitchen sinks, which we also made from discarded oil drums. Those sinks were large enough to submerge 10 gallon pots and pans in.

We engineered hot and cold running water for our kitchen sinks using materials we scrounged from the base salvage yard, by fabricating a water heater from three 55 gallon oil drums (photo on left) and a tower for water storage with gravity flow to the heater and the kitchen sinks.

Sinks with piped hot water were key to cleanliness in the kitchen.

Indoor cooking required venting of fumes to the outside, so I designed a vented cook stove which we constructed from a salvaged steel oil drum. The sterilizing tank, was also made from an oil drum. The design included a metal carrying basket to submerge table ware into the tank. The combustion chamber is underneath the tank.

I had watched and learned from my father on the farm growing up. He was always inventing equipment or tools to get the job done, using his intellect and his great mechanical aptitude to fabricate equipment and tools. I like to think that I was following in his footsteps, when I designed and constructed many useful mess hall items out of military salvage yard materials.

In the foreground of the above photo is the cook stove I designed from an oil drum, and below, the sterilizing tank is visible on the left side of the photo. Both the cook stove and the sterilizing tank were fueled with wood and/or coal. We installed venting pipes from the fuel burning compartments on both items to allow for indoor use.

COOKING EXPERIMENTS

THE THIRD PART of my food service training seminar was all about the food. There is no doubt about it, in my mind, government issued food stuffs are of good quality and nutritious, however, making some of the war time government issue preserved foods palatable was a challenge. However, when properly prepared and cooked, using a little imagination, reconstituted and canned military chow, in those remote military camps, could look and taste as appetizing and appealing as mom's home cooked meals.

My experimentation with standard military issue food products was spurned in January, 1944, after a four day flight from the U.S.A., via South America, Ascension Island and North Africa. The morning after I arrived in India. I got up for breakfast, exhausted from the trip, and not quite awake. I was promptly served scrambled green eggs and spam.

The canned spam (a mixture of salty pork and beef) was tasty enough, but, the green eggs were not the least bit tasty or appetizing to look at. They were made from government issue dehydrated eggs which would turn green shortly after being cooked. YUK! I have often wondered if such an encounter is what inspired Dr. Seuss to write the children's book, "Green Eggs and Ham." Maybe he, too, served as a soldier overseas during WWII.

Not long after eating those memorable green eggs, I was once again (against my wishes) assigned duty as Mess Officer, in charge of some mess halls that were serving (you guessed it) those same yucky green eggs. Taking matters into my own hands, I began to experiment with alternative methods to prepare and cook the powdered eggs--hoping to solve the color and taste dilemma.

After several experiments, using a variety of ingredients available in the military mess halls (condiments, seasonings, herbs, spices, extracts, etc.), I developed a select combination which, when cooked together with the powdered eggs, significantly delayed the onset of greenish discoloration and resulted in significantly better tasting scrambled eggs.

My quick success with the scrambled egg recipe for the troops in my mess sparked my enthusiasm to find other uses for those dehydrated eggs. After more experimentation, my hunch was validated, dehydrated eggs could be blended very successfully into many recipes, especially cakes, puddings and pancakes. One of my recipes, a fruit-nut-spice cake, soon became a favorite with the troops.

And spam--oh yes, abundant quantities of canned spam were forever being issued from the Quartermaster (supply unit). Of course, the mess halls kept on serving it, weeks on end. Spam, though tasty, soon wore out its welcome on the menu, like too much of any food item, particularly if it is always prepared exactly the same. So, it was back to the kitchen to test and develop a variety of palatable "canned spam" recipes. The tests resulted in many new ways to better utilize spam and reduce the troops acquired aversion to the item. One of my recipes which became a favorite with the troops, was a spam casserole made with powdered potatoes, dehydrated onions and canned mixed vegetables.

Assisted by the Kunming AF Base Mess Officer, Mess Sergeants and cooks, and utilizing recipes I had previously developed for the troops, we trained fifty or so seminar attendees (officers and NCO's). The trainees observed meal planning, preparation and serving breakfast, dinner and supper for two consecutive days. All of the meals we prepared as part of the training demonstration seminar used Army Quartermaster issue foodstuffs, primarily dehydrated and canned food, supplemented when possible with locally produced vegetables and fresh meats.

The seminar ended with a specially prepared evening supper, with the Base Commander and his key staff officers attending as invited guests. The training seminar had been a great success. All expressed amazement and appreciation for our transformation of those dehydrated and canned foods into such an attractive and palatable (almost gourmet quality) meal.

The day after the seminar ended, my team of technicians and I departed Kunming, China to resume our regular food service training tour of U.S. Air Force bases in China.

FOOD SERVICE
TRAINING TOUR COMPLETED

ON AUGUST 16, 1945, while conducting an inspection, the base commander received a message from Hq. ICD-ATC Calcutta, India, that Japan had surrendered August 15, 1945. A couple of weeks later, at another air base, we were informed that the surrender documents were signed September 2, 1945, on the American Battleship Missouri.

WHOOPEE--HOORAY!!THE WAR WAS OVER!!!!!

On October 29, 1945, our four man inspection team had completed Food Service inspections of all the ATC Air Bases in China, Burma and India (CBI). As a team, the four of us had spent almost one year inspecting food service and supply functions and training personnel at U.S. (ATC) Air Force Bases in CBI. With the war over, we happily packed our gear and flew from China back to Hq. ATC, Calcutta, India.

For that assignment, I was awarded the Commendation Medal for outstanding performance of duty. I submitted a letter to Hq ATC recommending that the three sergeants on my training team be considered for the award of Commendation Medal for their outstanding performance on that long and arduous training mission.

On, November 2, 1945, I was reassigned to Hq. India China Division, Air Transport Command (ICD-ATC), Calcutta, India, with a new duty as Assistant Supply Services Officer. On January 1, 1946, I received a promotion to Major, with a reassigned duty as Chief of the Supply Services Division. A short time later, I submitted a request for transfer to Hq. ATC in Paris, France. The war with Japan had already ended, and I was ready for a change of scene and new adventures.

1350TH ATC BU, KUNMING, China.—**Captain Edward A. Trautt**, of Superior, is pictured above with his mobile mess team of the India China division of the air transport command.

His team has received many commendations for their superior work in improvising and constructing all types of mess equipment from salvaged material for all ATC mess halls in China.

Pictured above, from left to right, are Tech. Sgt. "Bud" Borden, Capt. Trautt, Master Sgt. "Swede" Hickman and Tech. Sgt. Stephen Herman.

DINING WITH THE KING OF SIAM

WITH WORLD WAR II ENDED IN EUROPE (Victory in Europe, V.E. Day, May 8, 1945) and in Asia (Victory in Japan, V.J. Day, August 15, 1945), I was assigned the additional duty of airplane trips from Hq. ATC, Calcutta, India to Burma, Siam (now Thailand), Malaya and Indochina, to coordinate the processing and return of American prisoners of war who were being released from Japanese Prisoner of War (POW) Camps in those countries.

Between November, 1945, and January, 1946, I made several trips to Rangoon, Mandalay, Bangkok, Saigon and Singapore. On one of those trips, in late January, 1946, I had a two day stopover in Bangkok, Siam. During that stopover, I accompanied three other officers on a sight-seeing tour of the city of Bangkok. I was very surprised to find so many taxi drivers, merchants and government officials who spoke English.

Our group toured the city of Bangkok by taxi and then about mid-day we visited Siam's famous temple of the Emerald Buddha. On an altar inside the temple was the world's largest block of green jade, carved into a statue of the sitting Buddha. Close by hung a huge circular brass alloy plate, a few feet in diameter. Pointed directly at the center of the plate was a large hanging wooden pole. That apparatus was used as a bell or gong for special Buddhist religious ceremonies. The operator could produce appropriate sounds for special ceremonies, sounds ranging from very low soft tones to extremely loud.

We found the temple nearly filled with mid-day worshipers, quietly meditating. As we passed by the gong, an Army Air Force Captain in our group just couldn't resist the devilish temptation to wham the gong. He pulled the ramming pole way back and slammed it into the gong plate, producing an extremely loud shrill vibrating, ear piercing sound. Everyone in the temple instantly covered their hurting ears with their hands and stared in shock at the four American officers, who were also covering their ears. Instantly, pandemonium broke out as everyone, ears still covered, rushed in panic for the nearest exit.

In this photo, I am second from the left. It was taken during the site-seeing tour in Bangkok when the captain (on the far right) committed the insult of banging the gong in the temple. When he did it, he had a silly guilty grin on his face, and the rest of us were totally bewildered by his brazen disrespect for the temple worshipers.

Being the senior officer in the group, it was my responsibility to reprimand the Captain for his childish and insensitive action. As our group exited the temple, I did reprimand him and I told him that if he was half as smart as he thinks he is, he would catch the first bus or taxi back to the airport before the offended crowd decided to teach him a lesson in oriental retribution for his stupid behavior.

The Captain did indeed return to the airport and I expressed my desire to the other officers to continue the temple visit. They decided to continue a tour of the city and departed. Just as I turned to reenter the temple, a distinguished looking local Siamese gentleman approached me, introduced himself and said he overheard what I told the Captain and the other American officers. I requested that he accept my apology for my companion's inconsiderate action. He then asked if I would like to see more of the temple. For about the next half hour, he escorted me through the temple, explaining its history, especially that of the statue of the sitting Emerald Buddha. Later, he shared some of the history of the country. It seems, that during the 19th century, Siam survived amid British, French and Dutch imperialism as an independent state. In December 1941, Siam's strongman, Premier Pipul Souggram, threw the country's lot with Japan. Japan then used the country as a strategic base in World War II until it surrendered to America in September 1945. The United States, long friendly toward Siam, restored Siamese assets which had been seized by Japan and other nations during the war and, on January 5, 1946, reaffirmed the Treaties of 1927 and 1937.

After our tour of the temple, the Siamese gentleman and I stopped at a nearby tea house for refreshments. Over tea, we discussed our respective country's customs, families, schools, etc. He spoke fluent English, which he had learned initially in high school from an imported British instructor. If I remember correctly, he said he was a graduate of a United States medical school, the Johns Hopkins Medical University in Baltimore, Maryland, U.S.A. When I met him, he was the Director of Public Health for Siam. I guess I'm finally getting old, after these almost 50 years since that chance meeting, I cannot for the life of me recall his name.

As we were about to finish our tea, the doctor asked if I would like to visit the Royal Palace and possibly the King, if he wasn't about some task of state. So, off we went to the Palace, what an oriental splendor and magnificence, a living fairytale!

Would you believe it, yes, I met the King, "Ananda Mahidol," who was preparing for an afternoon session with the National Legislature. The King spoke French and English. He invited me to accompany the Health Director to the meeting. Prior to the legislature meeting which was scheduled for mid-afternoon, the doctor gave me a tour of the Palace. I accompanied him to the legislative chambers and we were ushered to seats only a few persons away from the King. After the usual opening of the session, the speaker introduced a couple of visiting foreign dignitaries and then me, as an American Air Force Officer on an official military mission to Siam coordinating the processing of American POW's being released by the Japanese. The session lasted about two hours.

After the legislature session ended, the doctor and I accompanied the King and a retinue of eight legislators to the imperial gardens. The King gave a short speech to the multitude of loyal subjects gathered there. He then walked through the hundreds gathered on the palace grounds, greeting all as he passed. As the King walked through the crowd, those being approached would all squat or kneel down, arising only after the King had passed. It was explained to me that this action was required for security reasons.

After about an hour, the King, his 8 legislators, the doctor and I returned to the palace. A group of about ten government officials, waiting for the King's return, joined the King and our entourage for a royal Siamese feast of oriental foods and wines. Ever so often, I would pinch myself to see if it was for real, or was I dreaming?

During the festivities and the honor of dining with the King of Siam, I was introduced to several Siamese and foreign dignitaries. The two I remember best were the Chiefs of the Department of Education and the Department of Health. They described the education system in Siam and questioned me about the U.S. education system and my field of study, etc. After considerable discussion, I was asked if I would be interested in accepting a position of teaching high school chemistry and maybe English in Bangkok, Siam, after I completed my military obligation. The position included a house and salary about double what I could have earned at the time teaching in the U.S.A. My reply was to let me think about it for a while and on a subsequent trip we could discuss the plan again. I was given the name and address of the Chief of the Department of Education, just in case I might be interested.

While in Bangkok, the fabulous oriental dinner, which I attended with the King of Siam, was only one of several other great dinners that I was privileged to attend on special occasions during my Air Force foreign duty assignments in Europe, North Africa, Middle East and the Orient. I thoroughly enjoyed the wide variety of fine ethnic foods served at those dinners, the foods were often exotic beyond belief to me. Remember, I was born and raised on farms in the mid-west where meat, potatoes and bread were the staples.

That trip to Bangkok, Siam in late January, 1946, shortly after the end of World War II, was my last trip to Siam. On January 31, 1946, my request for transfer to Europe was approved. A few days after returning to Hq. ICD-ATC, Calcutta, India, from Bangkok, Siam, I was transferred to Hq. European Division, Air Transport Command (EURD-ATC), Paris, France.

PART 6

FRANCE ASSIGNMENT

PARIS ASSIGNMENT
Rest and Recuperation Leave

I ARRIVED AT MY NEW ASSIGNMENT in Paris, France, on February 5, 1946, and was assigned to duty as Assistant Supply-Services Officer. A few days later I began inspecting the Food Service and Base Exchange facilities at ATC Army Air Force Bases in Europe and North Africa. Within a couple of weeks, I was approved for a 45 day rest and recuperation (R&R) leave, plus travel time, to my home in Superior, Wisconsin. I had not seen my family since December, 1943, more than two years.

On February 13, 1946, at Herbert Tereyton (LeHavre, France), I boarded a U.S. Navy Troop transport ship (Kaiser Liberty)--destination Fort Hamilton, Brooklyn, New York, U.S.A. On that first day at sea, I went to the officers mess for breakfast. There in the food serving line was Staff Sergeant Mickey Rooney, doing K.P. duty. In disbelief, I said to him, "Not, the Mickey Rooney?!" "Sure am." he replied. After everyone was served, I spoke to Mickey for a few moments, as I did on several occasions later. Mickey was a real trooper, always friendly, with a joke to tell.

From Brooklyn I travelled by train to Fort Sheridan, Illinois, where I was issued the orders for a 45 day R&R leave, so that I could spend time with my family at their home at 2608 East 7th Street (East End), Superior, Wisconsin.

I was finally visiting home from the war, after serving more than two years overseas during WWII. Unbeknownst to me, when soldiers returned home from overseas duty, the Red Cross notified their parents in advance. I had hoped to surprise my parents by arriving home unannounced. Not so, they had been advised by the Red Cross of the date and time of my arrival.

What a homecoming that was! As my taxi drove up in front of my home – there stood my mom and dad, on the front porch, excitingly waving then running to the taxi. Mom, with tears of joy, was first to hug me, then dad. When I left for the war, my inexperience and childhood were left behind, I returned home now, as a mature adult, innocence lost.

I asked if any other family members were home. They replied, "Let's go inside and phone everyone that you're home—but first, you must see our beautiful spring garden. Lo and behold, the garden was crowded with family members, some of my college friends, and neighbors. All yelled at the top of their voices, "Welcome home!!"

What a party that was, renewing old acquaintances and then telling my parents and family my war story. I spent the following month visiting everyone, even dating some girls from my college days (nothing serious).

Two days before my 31st birthday, on April 27, 1946, before my return trip to Paris, France, mom and dad threw a combination birthday/going away party for me with family and special friends. My visit was wonderful, but departing was sad, I was leaving my home and family again, not knowing when I would return.

Two days later, on my birthday, I reported back to Fort Sheridan to receive my return orders directing me to Camp Kilmore, New Jersey, to board a Navy ship for the return voyage to France. The accommodations on that voyage were a wonderful surprise. The ship was a former Italian pleasure cruise ship that was captured during the war. The passenger list included a National Guard Group (Special Services) from LeMars, Iowa, where I had attended school from 7th grade through 10th grade. Several of the group were brothers or sisters of my former LeMars classmates. During the entire voyage the weather was great, the food was plentiful and delicious and each evening after dinner, we danced to a live military band. Also, at each base stopover, the military provided live stage shows with Hollywood movie stars.

Upon arrival in France, I was informed that my Paris unit had been relocated at Bremen, Germany, and I was ordered to proceed on to that destination. However, when I arrived in Bremen, I found that there had been a mix-up and my Air Force unit was still in Paris after all. Finally, I arrived at my Hq. in Paris and resumed my Air Force inspection duties.

I really enjoyed that assignment, especially the extensive travel it required to U.S. Air Force Bases in Europe and North Africa, and because I was finally assigned to something other than food service.

For my next assignment, I hoped I would have the opportunity to continue on a path other than food service functions. But it was not to be, my subsequent assignment, for the third time since I joined the military, was again filling another food service position. The personnel officer informed me that it was an emergency, they needed me to fill a vacancy in food service at Orly Air Field, Paris.

I pleaded to remain in my Hq. Staff job, but to no avail. It was a done deal, Colonel Sarry Smith, Orly Field Commander, had requested me for the job and the Hq. EURD-ATC Commanding General had already approved the move. I guess, like all good soldiers, mine was "not to reason why. . ." So, on October 16, 1946, I reported to Orly Field where I was assigned the duty of Base Food Service Officer and Officer in charge of the Hotel Napoleon Bonaparte, the ATC billets, Officers Club and dining room for ATC officers stationed in Paris.

In the meantime, I was considering the lucrative teaching opportunity offered to me by the Siam Chief of the Department of Education. However, as tempting as the offer was, as yet, I was still undecided. I communicated that by letter to the Siam Department of Education. I received an unexpected reply in July, 1946, informing me that, the previous month, King Mahidol had been found shot dead in his own bed in his Bangkok palace under mysterious circumstances. Mahidol was almost 21 years old when he died. Later his death was ruled a murder and three servants were executed. I did not pursue the Siam teaching position further.

In early July, 1946, when office routine was less hectic than usual, I casually asked my French secretary if she knew a respectable, unattached young lady who might be interested in attending dinner dances with me at our Officers Club. She promised to check with friends.

A couple of times a week, I would ask her if she had talked to anyone yet. Yes, she had, but most of her friends seemed to be unavailable.

Then one day, she showed me a picture of Ludmila and two of her friends and asked if I would be interested in meeting any of them. Without hesitation, I selected Ludmila. "Wow," I said, "She's the one I want to meet!"

Ludmila is on the right, with two friends.

Later, after Ludmila and I were engaged, my secretary gave me this photo to keep.

As luck would have it, one rainy day, to stay dry, the young lady in the photo had left her bike at my secretary's house and took the metro (subway train) home instead. She would have to pick up her bike sometime soon and then my secretary would have the chance to ask her about accompanying me to the Officers Club dinner dances. Almost every day, I asked the secretary if she had seen her friend yet. Every day the answer was the same, no, not yet.

Finally, later that month, the day I had been waiting for arrived. My secretary came rushing into my office, smiling. She told me her friend Ludmila had come by for her bike and would like to meet me and attend Officers Club dances and especially wanted the opportunity to practice her English.

Being a good and efficient secretary, she made the arrangements for the "WOW" girl on the photograph to meet me at my office. As it turned out, she worked as a secretary in Paris, only a short walking distance from our Hotel Military Headquarters.

I will never forget that day, I received a telephone call shortly before office closing time, from the military guard at the front entrance gate to our headquarters, asking if I had an appointment with a Ludmila Perebaskine. Expecting her, I said, "Yes, send her up to my office, please." My office was on the second floor and opened onto the mezzanine, overlooking the hotel's front door and the large lobby below.

There she was, a perfect image of the girl of my dreams, an elegant young lady coming through the main entrance door. She hesitated and looked around, I imagined she was a little bewildered by all the military formality and security. Hesitantly, she proceeded across the lobby and headed for the long stairs to the second floor. At the same time, I started down the stairs to meet her. As she came walking across the lobby, she appeared more beautiful than her photograph. She was dressed so neatly in a very pretty dress, red and white shoes, a light beige spring coat and a beautiful shy blushing smile. It was the end of the workday on Friday, the beginning of the weekend.

I left my office and escorted Ludmila to the Hotel Napoleon Bonaparte for dinner. Over dinner, we planned a full evening of fun and laughter, for a night out in the big city of Paris. After dinner, we saw a movie and then went for a stroll down the from the Arc de Triumph on the beautiful Champs-Elysees, a famous street in the center of Paris.

After window shopping for a while, we stopped at a sidewalk café where we sampled beverages and out of this world French pastries. Paris is well known for its sidewalk cafes, eating at one can be quite an experience. The large assortments of exquisite and delicious desserts, food and beverages on the menus, were astonishing.

Earlier in the day, I had picked up a couple of candy bars at the Base Exchange. While we were window shopping, I gave Ludmila one bar. We continued walking, talking and window shopping. I noticed Ludmila took one small bite of the bar and discretely put in her coat pocket. A little while later, I asked her if she would like another candy bar. She said yes, and as we walked and talked and window shopped, she took only one little bite of the bar and also put it in her pocket. At the time, I sort of wondered--maybe she was saving it for later.

After an exciting evening in beautiful, romantic Paris, I took Ludmila home (about 45 minutes by Metro). Before saying goodnight, I asked her if she would accompany me on a sightseeing tour of Paris the next day. On that second date, I brought up the subject of the candy bars I had given her the night before. Blushing shyly, she told me she had taken them home to share with her family. That small act of generosity and thoughtfulness touched my soul. The night before, on our first date, I already thought I was falling in love. Less than 24 hours after meeting Ludmila, especially after she told me what she had done with the candy bars, I knew I was smitten.

Ludmila gave me this photo of her on our third date. It was taken a few weeks before we met. The photo of me in uniform was taken about this same time. On our fourth date, I gave Ludmila this photo of me.

We dated several days each week after that first weekend, always having a wonderful time. We went sightseeing in and around Paris, visiting scenic gardens, historical monuments, art museums and attending operas. There were also occasions when I took Ludmila and her family to dinner at the U.S. Air Force Officer's Club in the Hotel Napoleon.

Shortly before I met Ludmila, I had enrolled in an Air

Force conversational French class. After we started dating, Ludmila and I discussed how we could help each other with our language skills. We decided that I would speak French to her and she, in turn, would speak English to me. I found myself struggling to speak French with some semblance of correctness. In comparison, Ludmila would speak to me in fluent, grammatically correct English, with very distinct British and Russian accents. The accent was due to speaking Russian as her native tongue and learning English in her teen years from a British high school teacher. Because Ludmila spoke English with both accents, I had difficulty understanding her at first and sometimes asked her to repeat herself.

I do not have an aptitude for languages and I found it especially difficult to pronounce many tongue twister French words. Consequently, Ludmila, as well as my French instructor, had many good laughs listening to my mispronounced words. By the time we became engaged, my French grammar had improved somewhat and my pronunciation elicited considerably fewer laughs.

On a visit to Ludmila's home, I expressed some curiosity about French schools and asked Ludmila what the diplomas actually looked like. Ludmila found some of her report cards and a diploma. She was on the honor roll and excelled in all subjects, with outstanding grades in math and languages (Russian, French, German and English). Not only is she beautiful, but intelligent, too!

From August through September, 1946, I visited Ludmila very often at her home and sometimes at homes of her relatives. During one of the visits, I learned that Ludmila's parents were White Russians who escaped from St. Petersburg, communist Russia, and now were refugees living and working in Paris. From the very beginning of our acquaintance, Ludmila was never pretentious, but rather always an elegant and vivacious young lady. It didn't take long for me to know for sure that I was in love with her.

Within two months of meeting Ludmila, I had made up my mind to marry her if she would have me.

Ludmila and I, visiting with her aunts and uncles

Ludmila and I with her mother and stepfather in the foreground,
and her sister and cousin the left side of the photo.

PLANS FOR MARRIAGE

ON OCTOBER 3rd, 1946, I submitted a letter to Hq. EURD-ATC, Paris, France, requesting permission (military requirement) to marry my new found love–the one and only, lovely and beautiful Ludmila Perebaskine. Ooops!!! Only, I had not yet asked Ludmila about it--I hadn't even proposed!

When I finally did approach her about marriage, my message wasn't clear to Ludmila. I was afraid to say the specific words, "Will you marry me?" What if she wouldn't be willing to leave her family and home in Paris? What if she said no?

Time was running out, so, one day, when I got the nerve to ask her to marry me, instead of using the word "marry", I asked her if she would come with me to my pending assignment in Germany. When she didn't respond, I was really perplexed, and apparently, so was Ludmila. Later, when she didn't show up for a meeting we had planned, I was distraught and bewildered beyond belief.

I wondered why she failed to show. My older and more experienced friend who was my secretary, and who also had introduced me to Ludmila, knew how much I loved Ludmila, and offered advice to help me patch up the problem. She recommended that I present Ludmila with a white carnation, the national flower of France. My French secretary told me that the flower symbolizes sweetness, loveliness, innocence, pure love, faithfulness, fascination and passion. Its symbolism was precisely how I felt about Ludmila, the love of my life.

Two weeks later, I received military approval to marry Ludmila Perebaskine, the wonderful and lovely girl of my dreams. This time, I still didn't actually ask Ludmila to marry me, I simply told her that I received a letter of approval from Command Headquarters to marry her!! Surprised, she said "I didn't know--but that's fine. We need now to prepare for the wedding and firm up dates, places and announcements."

Gosh, it's amazing how I got all the way through the wedding without actually asking Ludmila to marry me, other than informing her that Headquarters had granted me permission to marry her. It was actually a close call, though I didn't realize it at the time, I almost missed the boat with Ludmila. It was one blunder I will have to chalk up to country-kid ignorance. I guess it's just the luck of the Irish! Ludmila explained to me later how close I came to losing her, and how I won back her heart. At my request she wrote her story in the next chapter.

THE OTHER SIDE OF THE STORY
by Ludmila

AFTER SPENDING ABOUT TEN DAYS in the country at my aunt's house where Edward joined me for a week-end, I returned to Paris where I found a very nice letter from Edward. We had a slight misunderstanding of which he wasn't even aware, due to his failure to propose at the right time, so I had almost decided we should go our separate ways. Then I read the letter, he was asking me to meet him in the lobby of the Hotel Napoleon, a fancy French hotel requisitioned by the American forces and of which Edward was put in charge. When I arrived at the hotel, I came in through a side entrance, instead of the main entrance where Edward was awaiting me with a clear view of the front door.

I walked through the entire lobby but did not find him, so I finally decided to leave a note for him at the desk. I don't know how I missed him for he waited for me for two hours. I left feeling this was not meant to be. In the meantime, Edward was moving to a different hotel, besides he did not get the note which, incidentally, followed him much later to his new address.

Come Monday, each of us was at work at our respective work places. Edward did not know what to do, so his secretary suggested he should call me at work, try to make a date and then give me a white carnation, the meaning of which I was supposed to understand. The day of the date Edward had difficulty acquiring the flower because his French chauffeur refused to understand his somewhat mis-pronounced French.

I left work and proceeded on foot on the Champs-Elysees, one of the large avenues which converge, like spokes on a wheel, on the Place de l'Etoile and the Arc de Triomphe. At quitting time the avenue was especially crowded, and Edward, not wanting to miss me this time, perched himself on the concrete railing at the entrance of the metro, something no self-respecting Frenchman would ever think of doing. So, there was Edward, in his American Air Force uniform, holding a white carnation, the meaning of which every passing Frenchman understood, but which totally escaped me. It wasn't the flower but the whole scene that touched me, Edward reminded me of a shy school-boy with his sweet smile.

That evening, Ed still didn't ask me if I would marry him, instead, he proposed to me by informing me that the papers had been approved by his military Headquarters permitting us to be married. That night I took the good news to my family, that we were engaged.

Major E. A. Trautt Married in Paris

Major Edward A. Trautt, son of Mr. and Mrs. John J. Trautt of 19 East Penning, Wood River, and Miss Ludmila Perebaskine, were married Dec. 8, in an elaborate Russian rite ceremony in Paris. The Russian ceremony was preceded by a civil courts ceremony on Dec. 7, and followed by a ceremony in a Catholic church. Major Trautt, a native of Iowa, has been in the army for seven years, enlisting before the outbreak of the war. He was one of six children of Mr. and Mrs. Trautt in the service during World War II. His parents moved to Wood River last May from Superior, Wis. A brother, Staff Sgt. Norbert W. Trautt, is stationed at Scott Field.

Major Trautt's bride is a linguist, and was employed in Paris when she met Major Trautt.

Following a tour of duty in Germany, and a trip to Italy during which they will visit Vatican City, Major Trautt and his bride will come to Wood River to visit his parents. They expect to make the trip to Wood River next June.

MARRIED IN PARIS

ON OCTOBER 15, 1946, Hq. ATC-Paris approved my request for permission to marry Ludmila. That same evening she took the news home to her family that we were engaged. Preparations for our wedding began immediately. Her mother found a beautiful wedding gown and arranged for a church wedding. She also found a great bargain on a diamond engagement ring and gold wedding bands for each of us. I made the arrangements for the reception and the wedding dinner-ball.

Less than two months later, we were married three times. French Law required a civil wedding, which was held on December 7, 1946. Then, two church weddings, one for Ludmila's family, a Russian Orthodox marriage on December 8th, followed by a Catholic marriage for my religious beliefs, on December 27, 1946.

Our Russian marriage ceremony was held, during high mass, at the Russian Orthodox Church, located at 57 Alexandre Nevsky, Paris on December 8, 1946.

After the wedding ceremony at the Russian Orthodox Church, (above photo), we celebrated with a dinner reception in the large ornate ballroom at the Hotel Napoleon Bonaparte in Paris (below).

To satisfy the epicurean tastes of the polyglot gathering, specially prepared Russian, French and American foods were served. The occasion was liberally interspersed with Russian caviar, vodka, French champagne and cognac and American (California Napa Valley) wines. A live band played Russian, French, and American music during dinner and afterward for dancing.

We took up temporary residency in the Hotel Napoleon Bonaparte after our Russian wedding and a few days later we departed Paris on the first part of our honeymoon, for a two week sightseeing tour of the scenic wonders of France and Germany.

When we returned to Paris after the first part of our honeymoon trip, we had our third marriage ceremony, this time in the Catholic Church. Afterward, we then resumed our honeymoon and departed Paris by train for a week long extended honeymoon in Switzerland and Italy. The Alps mountains were a beautiful winter wonderland. In Rome, we joined with 10,000 others to receive a communal blessing from Pope Pious XII during his daily appearance from a balcony of his residence and we visited the Vatican and St. Peters Cathedral.

Ludmila and I, ready to board the train on our continued honeymoon trip, this time to Switzerland and Italy.

Left to right: Ludmila's cousin Vladimir Ziloff, Aunt Anna, Aunt Tatiana, Ludmila and I.

After our return to Paris and a few days rest at our apartment in the Hotel Napoleon Bonaparte, I returned to duty at Orly Airport. On the first day back to work, in mid-January, 1947, the Base Commander, Colonel Sarry Smith, a graduate of West Point, reminded me that the closing date to apply for a Regular Army Commission was only a few days away and encouraged me to apply. Two months later, I still had not applied, and with only a couple of days left before the application deadline, Col. Smith called me into his office. Uh oh, now what, I wondered. As I entered his office, he sternly informed me that he had not received my application for

Regular Army and asked if I was still interested. My reply--
yes, sir. "O.K! Then fill out these forms." he ordered.

I filled out the forms then and there and handed them back
to the Colonel. He smiled, shook my hand and told me he was
attaching a letter highly recommending me for a Regular
Commission. Then, without further ado, he looked me in the
eye and sternly said, "Now, get your procrastinating butt
down to the personnel office and arrange for travel orders.
The following morning, I flew to Hq. USAF, Wiesbaden,
Germany to take tests for a Regular Army Commission. I
spent that afternoon and the next two days in interviews and
taking written and oral exams. They told us we would receive
the test results by June. Upon my return, I was happy to
report back to Colonel Smith that I had completed the written
tests in record time and that the oral interviews seemed to
have gone well. On March 12, 1947, my tour of duty in
Europe ended, and I was reassigned to Hq. 503 Air Force Base
Unit (AFBU), Bolling Field, Washington, D.C.

In our temporary quarters at the Hotel Napoleon Bonaparte.

Before departing for the U.S.A. for my next duty assignment, I accompanied Ludmila's immediate family (stepfather, mother and sister) to the American Embassy in Paris to file applications for immigration to the U.S.A. After completing their applications, I was informed that the waiting period would probably be about two to three years.

PART 7

RETURN HOME
TO AMERICA
AFTER THE END OF WW II

AMERICAN SOLDIER RETURNS HOME
WITH BRIDE

ON APRIL 18, 1947, my beautiful, young Russian bride and I departed Paris, France by train for the ocean port of Bremerhaven, Germany, en route to the good old U.S.A. Three days later, we departed Bremerhaven on a U.S. Navy troop ship (Kaiser Liberty Ship).

Enjoying the open air deck
on the Kaiser Liberty Ship.

After passage through the North Sea, past the White Cliffs of Dover, through the English Channel and onward for seven more days riding out the very rough and stormy Atlantic Ocean, we arrived at Fort Hamilton, Brooklyn, New York, U.S.A. on April 29, 1947, my 32nd birthday.

HONEYMOON HEAVEN

AFTER CLEARING THROUGH port customs at Fort Hamilton, Brooklyn, New York, we traveled by subway to New York City and checked into Hotel Lincoln shortly before noon. We ate lunch and then hurried to Times Square and walked up and down the street window shopping and gawking in awe at all the tall buildings and crowds of people hurrying about.

After some time of oooohhhing, aaahhhing, gawking and window shopping, we noticed an elderly, distinguished-looking gentleman who appeared to be staying purposefully in close proximity. We were young, enthusiastic, interested in everything around us and intoxicated with love. The gentleman had followed us for a while, staying within hearing distance. Eventually, he approached us with a very friendly "Hello". He asked us if we were enjoying our visit to New York City and questioned us about where we were from, whether we had been in New York before and why we were here. We told him we had met in Paris after the war and that we were now on our honeymoon and I would soon return to my military duties.

After a few more questions, the gentleman asked if we would like to stay at the Waldorf-Astoria Hotel while visiting in New York City. I said that only a few minutes ago we had checked into the Hotel Lincoln, and again he asked, "Well, would you still like to stay at the Waldorf?"

I replied, "We'd probably lose our deposit if we checked out now." We didn't know anything about the man, but he sure seemed very interested in us staying at the Waldorf.

"I see you're an Air Force Officer, he said. "Go back to the Hotel Lincoln and tell the desk clerk that you can't take the room after all, because you were just notified that your unit was ordered to move out in just a few hours."

Then he said, "How about it, are you willing to do that?"

I leaned over to Ludmila and said, "I theenk we're about to buy the Brooklyn Bridge." Turning toward the old gent, "Okay," I agreed, "we'll try our luck on getting our deposit back--but first, what is your name, and who do we talk to at the Waldorf?"

His response, as he wrote a note on a piece of paper, was, "Here, give this to the desk clerk at the Waldorf."

I took the note and thanked him and we went back to the Lincoln Hotel. Wonders never cease! The desk clerk refunded our entire room deposit and then we checked out.

As we taxied to the Waldorf-Astoria, we read his note which simply stated, "Check the Major and his new bride into the usual accommodations." The note was signed with an illegible signature.

Off we went to the Waldorf-Astoria around 5:00 P.M. We presented the note to the desk clerk, he turned and called for the manager, who responded, "Oh yes, we have a room reserved for you, Major."

After he registered us and sent our luggage to our room, he gave us tickets to the hotel's stage show/dinner/dance that night and said, "Enjoy the evening, and I'll see you for brunch tomorrow morning between 9:00 and 11:00."

We rode the elevator umpteen floors up, found our room number and opened the door. Lo and behold! It was the HONEYMOON SUITE!!!!!! It came with a king size bed, hot, cold and chilled water faucets in the room, a corner bar, Crystal bowls filled with expensive candies and an assortment of fresh fruits and furniture fit for royalty. We had a snack, rested for a while, dressed for the occasion, and then took the elevator up to the dinner/show/dance. We danced until 11:00 P.M. and then returned to our suite, a little tired from our trip, the excitement of the evening and the dancing. We both were ready for some much needed rest. It didn't take long to fall asleep in that big, fluffy, billowy cloud of a bed, floating in a reality that was better than any dreamland.

April 30th, morning time. We got up, dressed and took the elevator to the first floor restaurant. After we were seated, the manager came to our table and presented us with tickets to a matinee performance at the Radio City Music Hall. After a big leisurely brunch, we took a taxi to the music hall. When we returned to the hotel around 5:00 or 6:00 P.M., guess what! The manager gave us two more tickets to the hotel's stage show dinner-dance. Again we danced until 11:00 P.M.

When we returned to our suite that night, we found new servings of a variety of delicious candies and fruits. Wow, what a birthday celebration that had turned into!!! We still couldn't believe it!!! A second night at the Waldorf in the honeymoon suite!!! We decided to spend the remainder of the evening just relaxing and enjoying the solitude of the suite. Finally, the sandman sprinkled our eyes with tiny sparkling stars and we fell fast asleep.

The following morning, May 1st, we again took the elevator down to brunch. We couldn't believe it, the manager gave us tickets to the Broadway stage show "Oklahoma." What a show that was, but it was another late evening before we could return to our honeymoon hotel heaven for much needed rest and sleep.

Morning, May 2nd, came too soon. It was time to pack and be on our way back to reality and my military assignment in Washington, D.C. We got dressed, packed our luggage, and took the elevator down to our last morning brunch at the Waldorf. We sure did enjoy that brunch--but, not knowing what was to be our next surprise, we checked our bank balance to make sure we had assets enough to pay for all the bills, thinking maybe we really did buy the Brooklyn Bridge and maybe more. Check out time approached, it was still forenoon.

We got up our courage, picked up our luggage and briskly walked up to the check out desk clerk and I boldly asked for the bill for the three nights stay in the Bridal Suite. As I waited patiently for the bill, the desk clerk called for the manager. When he arrived he said, "Oh, there's no bill, everything was taken care of by that grand old gentleman who you talked to on Times Square."

I asked for the name of the gentleman, so I could at least write and thank him for his kindness, friendliness and generosity. Although he knew his name, he said no, because that's the way he wants it. The manager then told us that the old gentleman was very wealthy. His wife had recently died and his children were grown and financially independent. So, now, being quite lonely, he would walk around Times Square, hoping to meet up with young friendly tourists in love, to converse with and welcome them to New York. He would vicariously select some of those friendly couples to the Honeymoon Suite at the Waldorf --with all the glamour and glitter of a night out in New York City.

The manager told us this gentleman indulged in this pastime regularly, and gave the same special treatment to other young couples almost every month. I asked the manager why he did it. He said it was because on his own first trip to the big city of New York, when he was young and newly married, a stranger had done the same for him and his new bride.

WHAT A STORY, HUH?! The best part about it is, "IT'S TRUE!"

BOLLING FIELD ASSIGNMENT
WASHINGTON D.C.

ABOUT MIDDAY, on May 2, 1947, Ludmila and I departed from our fantasy stay at the Waldorf-Astoria Hotel in New York City. We taxied from the Waldorf-Astoria to Grand Central Railway Station and departed by train for Bolling Field, Washington, D.C. Upon arrival, I reported to Bolling Field Base Personnel, where I requested and was granted an extended leave of 30 days vacation.

The following afternoon, Ludmila and I departed by train (Pullman sleeper accommodations) for the long trip to Wood River, Illinois to visit my parents. That was her first visit with my folks and her new in-laws. After a few days, we purchased a car and small camping trailer to visit the rest of the Trautt clan.

Ludmila in our 1942 Chevrolet that we purchased
while visiting my folks in Wood River.

Ludmila and I in our new camping trailer, with two of my brothers,
Steve on the left and Joseph on the right.

At the end of my leave, we returned to Wood River where Ludmila stayed with my folks, while I reported to duty at Bolling Field. On June 4, 1947, I was assigned to on-the-job-training (OJT) in the Staff Services and Supply Section for two weeks. In my spare time, I located a small apartment in nearby in Washington, D.C. Upon completion of OJT, I returned to Wood River to bring Ludmila home to our new apartment.

On June 27, 1947, I was reassigned to Hq. Bolling Field, for duty as Assistant Staff Supply Services Officer. A few days later, the Personnel Officer informed me that I had passed the test for a Regular Army Commission (the test that I had taken four months earlier in Hq. USAFE, Wiesbaden, Germany).

On July 26, 1947, President Harry S. Truman signed the National Security Act of 1947. The measure established an independent Air Force and placed the Army, Navy and Air

Force on an equal level under a civilian Secretary of Defense. Until September 18, 1947, the Department of the Air Force did not begin operating as a separate entity. I had been sworn into the Regular Army Air Force on August 6, 1947, with a commission as permanent 1st Lt. and active duty temporary Major, the war time rank I held at the time. The following month, to comply with the National Security Act, the Army Air Force became the U.S. Air Force, as an autonomous branch of the U.S. Defense Forces.

The day I received my regular commission, I also received new orders reassigning me to Hq. Pacific Division, Air Transport Command (PACD-ATC), Fairfield-Suisun Air Force Base, Fairfield, California, later known as Travis Air Force Base. Before departing for California, I visited a friend of mine, Lt. Col. Meyer, Personnel Records Officer at the Pentagon. He informed me that I passed the Regular Army Tests in the upper 3% of the 128,000 who took the exam.

OPPORTUNITY IN POLITICS

DURING THE SHORT TIME that I was stationed at Bolling Field, Washington, D.C., I met a former Air Force Officer friend, John Blatnik, from northern Minnesota. We had been stationed at Lincoln, Nebraska Army Air Field in 1943 and had lived in the base bachelor officer's quarters (BOQ). At that time, we were both First Lieutenants. We became quite good friends and often, during uneventful evenings and mealtimes, we discussed our plans for post war endeavors. John always expressed an interest in politics. I was primarily interested in returning to the University of Wisconsin to continue my studies in biochemistry.

John did, in fact, become a politician and I remained in the service. In July, 1947, he was a democratic congressional representative from northern Minnesota. I was a Major in the military and had just received a commission in the Regular Army Air Force.

One evening, John met with me for dinner at the Bolling Field Officer's Club. We reminisced over the good old days and then discussed our present careers. During that meeting, John invited me to lunch at the congressional dining room the following week. That luncheon date turned into quite an exciting occasion. I was given a tour of both houses of congress and introduced to about forty democratic congressional representatives and senators. After the tour, we went to the huge congressional dining room for lunch at a table seating me and nineteen very talkative democrats, a mixture of very important representatives and senators.

It seemed that I became the center of discussion. I was questioned about where I was from, my age, time in service, education, and political interest. Finally, I leaned over to John and commented that it seemed that I was being interviewed for a job. "Could be," he replied. By the time lunch was over, I am sure the group had enough information to write my biography.

After lunch, the group proceeded to a lounge. After everyone was comfortably seated, a senator from Texas, evidently with seniority, took the floor, introduced himself again, and wasting no time, spoke up loudly and clearly and said, "Major Trautt, it is the consensus of this group that you should be the Democratic congressional representative from northern Wisconsin in the upcoming election. Others, including John Blatnik, stated why they thought I should run.

Finally, I stood up and requested permission to say a few words. In a loud voice, I said, "Whoops, did I understand you correctly?--me to run for congressional representative. Do you gentlemen and ladies (there were two ladies in the group) know what a married major's pay is, and how little of that can be put into savings? Also, I studied physical sciences in college, not political or social sciences." Their response was, "no problem, campaign funds, speech writers, advisors, and a vehicle for travel would be provided." They asked me to think it over and to get back to John in a couple of days with my decision.

I took a few days to mull over that very tempting venture into that new and strange world of politics. After carefully considering the pros and cons, a regular Army Air Force commission in my pocket versus the possibility of the loss of an election, I made my decision to continue in my military career. That was the beginning and end of my political career.

DESTINATION CALIFORNIA

ON AUGUST 8, 1947, Ludmila and I departed Washington, D.C. by auto for Fairfield, California. At the time, Ludmila was in a family way, in every sense of the word, she was 7 ½ months pregnant and anxious to get to California. En route, we visited again with my folks in Wood River. While we were there, my youngest brother, Joseph, asked if we would take him to California to finish his last year of high school. Everyone agreed a change of school was a good idea, so Joseph accompanied us to California.

After three days of driving, we arrived at Fairfield, California and on August 13th, I reported to Fairfield-Suisun Army Air Force Base, for my duty assignment as Base Food Service Supervisor. We moved into on-base housing, "our first "home", and we enrolled Joe into 12th grade in Fairfield High School.

The following month, our first child, Ann Cecilia, was born at Fort Baker Army base, which was located at the north end of the Golden Gate Bridge.

Ann Cecilia with her mother, Ludmila.

The photo above was taken in our base housing at Fairfield AFB

PART 8

MASSACHUSETTS ASSIGNMENT

MASSACHUSETTS ASSIGNMENT

ON JUNE 10, 1948, almost a year after Ann was born, I was reassigned to Headquarters Atlantic Division, Military Air Transport Service, (Hq. ATLD-MATS), Westover AFB, Holyoke, Massachusetts. Ludmila and I had barely settled into our first home in California and we hated to leave, but we vowed to return someday, when I retired from the Air Force.

Ludmila, little baby Ann, and I with my brother Stephen and parents.

En route to the new assignment in Massachusetts, we stopped over in Wood River, Illinois, to visit with my parents and to drop off my brother Joseph, since he had completed high school as planned. After a few days visit, Ludmila, baby Ann and I resumed our drive to Westover Air Force Base, arriving there on July 9, 1948.

ARMED FORCES SEGREGATION ENDS
by Presidential Executive Order

ON JULY 26, 1948, President Harry S. Truman signed an executive order ending racial segregation in the Armed Forces. In October 1948, I was reassigned to duty as Commander of the Food Service Squadron, Westover.

Coinciding closely with the timing of that presidential order, my squadron was scheduled to move to new barracks and, also, the Base Personnel Officer was having difficulty with the assignment of 1st Lt. Metcalf, a graduate of Syracuse University, who happened to be a black officer. It seemed that none of the white commanders wanted him in their squadrons.

My squadron was about one-third black and two-thirds white soldiers. I believed that it might be beneficial and wise to have a black officer on the Squadron Administrative Staff. I specifically requested to have Lt. Metcalf assigned to my unit as Squadron Adjutant. The Personnel Officer was really surprised at my request, especially since several white officers were waiting for assignment as administrative staff officers and the fact that some units on base would not accept him voluntarily. He thought I must have made a mistake and asked me if I was aware that the officer was black. "Yes, indeed," I replied, "that is precisely why I want him, to assist me in the supervision and management of my planned integrated squadron."

My request was granted, and after Lt. Metcalf took over duty as Adjutant, he and I prepared a roster of the personnel assigned to each new barrack, one-third black, two-thirds white in each. What a great opportunity to integrate the troops before they realized what had transpired. Everything seemed to be going fine, until the following day when a white Technical Sergeant objected. He reported to my office to protest the new arrangements. He let me know that he was a Texan and that he would not live in the same barracks with black troops. After he completed his little spiel, I asked him if he had volunteered for military service. "Yes, sir," he said. I then told him that he had two choices. One, he could voluntarily comply with the written order of his Commander-in Chief, the President of the United States, or, two, he could request voluntary discharge from military service. In the meantime, he was to return to his duties and the assigned barracks arrangements, until he decided what his choice would be.

Well, after only a few days and the weekend to think it over, the Sergeant reported back to my office with his decision. First, he apologized for his previous uncomplimentary remarks about blacks. He also said that he and other white Noncommissioned Officers (NCO's) were getting along fine with the black NCO's. He said that he believed integration would eventually be successful and again apologized and said, "You know, Major, I now realize that you'll never really know if a change or new idea will work or not, unless you give it an honest try."

As Squadron Adjutant, Lt. Metcalf did an outstanding job assisting me in the administration of the squadron activities and functions. A short time after integration of the squadron, all seemed calm and normal and remained so for the remainder of my command of the squadron.

In August, 1949, I became aware of an on-base vacancy for a Squadron Executive Officer, which looked like my opportunity to maneuver myself out of the Food Service classification. I discussed my dilemma with Colonel J. E. Barzynski, Base Commander. He heartily agreed with me and on September 7, 1949, he directed the Personnel Officer to reassign me to the 1600 Air Transport Squadron, with duty as Executive Officer.

Upon my reassignment, the Wing Commander, Brigadier General Archie Olds paid me a high compliment at a Wing Hq. Staff Meeting for the successful integration of my previous Food Service Squadron. He also pointed out that it was the first squadron to be integrated in the Military Air Transport Service (MATS) and probably the entire Air Force.

FAMILY EVENTS

ALMOST NINE MONTHS after our arrival in Massachusetts, Mary Margaret, our second daughter, was born in Springfield, Massachusetts Hospital on April 7, 1949. We were now a family of four, pictured below.

In August, 1949, a few months after Mary was born, we learned that Ludmila's mother Olga, still living in Paris, was seriously ill with a disease known as "Charcot" which is endemic to the region of Kiev, Russia. Olga had vacationed in that region in her youth.

When we were first married, we had hoped to have Ludmila's family join us in the United States. Ludmila had not seen her mother since we left Paris more than two years before. An opportunity arose for me to visit Ludmila's mother and family In December 1949, while on an inspection tour of food service and base exchange service functions at ATC Air Force Bases in Germany and France.

During my visit, I accompanied Ludmila's sister Natalie to the American Embassy in Paris to check on the status of their applications for immigration to the U.S.A. I was informed that because Natalie was a French citizen by birth, her name would soon be on the approved quota. However, since their stepfather and mother were Russian citizens residing in France as refugees, their wait would probably be considerably longer. Unfortunately, my mother-in-law's illness was terminal and she died six months afterward, on May 4, 1950, at the age of 59.

On June 25th, 1950, North Korean forces invaded South Korea, starting the Korean War, the first significant armed conflict of the Cold War after the end of World War II. It was the result of the physical division of Korea by an agreement of the victorious Allies at the conclusion of the Pacific War at the end of World War II. South Korea was supported by the United Nations in the Korean war, particularly the United States. We watched the events closely, knowing there was a good chance I could be assigned to duty in Korea during the conflict.

Ludmila received her Certificate of Naturalization at the U.S. District Court in Boston, Massachusetts on July 11, 1950, and legally became a proud citizen of the United States of America.

Later that month, Ludmila's only sibling, Natalie, was granted approval to immigrate to the U.S. In mid-November, she traveled to New York by ship and moved in with us the following day.

On October 5, 1950, Irene Jane, our third child, was born in a Holyoke, Massachusetts hospital.

Natalie's arrival was fortuitous, because I received orders on January 31, 1951, to report to Camp Stoneman, California, for travel orders to Korea. So, the following month, we packed up and drove by auto from Massachusetts to California, with a short stopover in Wood River, Illinois to visit my parents. A few days after arriving in Sacramento we found and rented a house on Ravenwood Street in the Arden-Arcade area of Sacramento where Ludmila would wait one year for me to return from overseas duty in Korea.

Not only did Ludmila's sister Natalie stay with her during my absence while I was in Korea, but, her stepfather Eugene Rybaltovsky also joined them in April, 1951 after receiving his immigration approval. It was a relief to me to know that Natalie and Eugene would be there to help Ludmila with our children, while I was overseas.

Edward A. Trautt

PART 9

KOREA ASSIGNMENT

HQ. 5TH AIR FORCE - TAEGU, KOREA

ON MARCH 1, 1951, I departed on a flight from Travis AFB, arriving five days later at Headquarters, 5th Air Force (Hq. 5th AF) Taegu, Korea where I was initially assigned on-the-job-training (OJT) in the staff supply division. Two weeks later, I was assigned as Supply Liaison Officer to Hq. 8th Army, Taegu, Korea. My duty assignment was Petroleum-Ammunition Supply Officer in an Army Office at the Port of Pusan, Korea. It was my job to coordinate emergency/priority shipments of petroleum and ammunition to USAF bases in Korea. That was a real staff supply job and I really enjoyed it.

November 5, 1951, I was reassigned back to Hq. 5th AF, Taegu, Korea, Materiel Division with a duty assignment of Chief, Petroleum Supply Branch. That job included supervising petroleum stock levels in Korea and coordinating the shipments of petroleum products (POL) from the U.S.A. to Korea. I liked staff supply duties and requested reclassification to the Supply Career Field. In December, 1951, I was reclassified as a career Air Force Supply Officer, and the future looked promising. I remained assigned as Chief of the Petroleum Supply Branch of Hq. 5th AF until March 13, 1952, when I returned to the U.S.A. from Korea.

While assigned to Hq. 5th AF, I regularly ate my meals at the Officer's Club Mess. On several occasions, I noticed a black officer who was always sitting alone during each meal. One day, I stopped by his table and introduced myself, asking if I could join him. He seemed very surprised but quickly said, "Please do." I made it a habit, whenever I saw him sitting alone, to sit down at his table. After a while, I learned he was highly educated with a Ph.D. from a University in Chicago, Illinois. Our friendship grew and before long other officers began asking to join us, soon our group grew so large we needed to move to bigger tables. Eventually, my friend was not only accepted as a fellow officer at meal times, but also at social functions, on duty, and on routine military functions. Although the President ordered integration of the troops in 1948, one cannot legislate the elimination of prejudice. By 1951, attitudes in the military were barely and slowly beginning to change.

I had been at Hq. 5th AF for a few months when a Lt. Colonel arrived for assignment in my unit. I can't remember his name now, but we had been stationed together at my previous assignment at Westover AF Base. He was familiar with the problems I had ˙ encountered when complying with the President's order to integrate the troops at Westover AF Base. The Colonel and I worked together at Hq. 5th AF for only a few months when the time arrived for me to rotate to the U.S.A. for a stateside assignment. One day, while I was sorting out my desk in preparation for my return to the U.S. and reunion with my family, the Colonel and a few other officers came into my office. As they all stood there, he said that he had a few words to say before I departed. He complimented me on my attitude and the handling of the integration problem not only previously at Westover AF Base, but also at Hq. 5th AF.

He then walked over to my desk and loudly asserted, "Major Trautt, if each Air Force Base had but only one officer complying with the spirit and intent of the Presidential executive order on integration as you have done, the transformation from race segregation to integration could have been accomplished much sooner and with considerably less opposition and animosity." The other officers then responded with "aye, aye" and wished me a good voyage home and continued success in my military career. In reply, I thanked him for his sincere friendship, and told him I appreciated his kind and generous words. I stated that I tried to live by the golden rule in treating my fellow soldiers in the same manner as I would like to be treated.

I was transferred on March 13, 1952, from Hq. 5th AF in Korea to Higashi Fuchu, Japan, for processing and air transport back to the U.S.A., Travis AFB, Fairfield, California, for reassignment to Hq., Air Proving Ground Command, Eglin AFB, Fort Walton, Florida. One week later, after 13 months in Korea, I was on my way home to the good old U.S.A. to rejoin my wife and children in California. I arrived at Travis A.F.B, California on March 21, 1952. Home again, thank God!

WARTIME LOVE MISSIVES

WHILE STATIONED IN KOREA, I did not have telephone facilities available for communication with home, so I had to rely on slow mail to keep in touch. During the occasional lulls from the duties and rigors of war, my thoughts would always turn to my wife and our three little girls. Sometimes I used those forlorn moments to capture my feelings by writing poetry to my sweetheart, Ludmila.

You may find my words "corny" in today's vernacular, but they were spoken from the heart. Expressing myself in this manner kept me from going berserk during those lonely and difficult days separated for 13 months from Ludmila and my three children. On the following pages, you will find a compilation of some of those poems. They are all addressed to "Toussia" which is Ludmila's childhood nickname.

From Korea: March 10, 1951

Dear Toussia,

Just a few thoughts for the day.

From time immemorial, it has been a valid and sacred truth,
that beauty inflames love in the hearts of youth.

That love's fervent and affectionately yearning sigh,
striving for mutual companionship, shall never die.

That to be honest in love, sincerity to each must be done.
That until joined in the nuptial ceremony, in either won.

That once united in the Holy Sacrament of a joyous marriage,
does one until death part, heavenward in a golden carriage.

Your loving husband,
Edward

During my assignment in Korea, Ludmila sent me many family photographs which helped keep me from going berserk without my family for that long, lonely year. Some of those treasured photographs are included below. The children's dresses in both photos below were hand made by Ludmila.

From Korea: May 3, 1951 (after receiving the above photo)

Dear Toussia,

Your "Happy Birthday" photograph arrived two days before my birthday – now . . .

IN VAIN I LONG FOR YOU

Ludmila, though far away my dear, you're always near.
For, I'm ardently in love, with you and heaven above.
With your heart for me unfurled, you're my entire world.
Your lovely charms, perpetuate desires to be in your arms.

The love that you always give, will in my soul forever live.
Now that I know you dear, of your love I have no fear.
I know there is no other, that I want to be my children's mother.
With this happiness comes sorrow, of going off to war tomorrow.

To unknown lands far away, God willing, soon home to stay.
Until death, your love I'll hold, for sentimentally my heart is bold.
We in love chose married life, war destined it loneliness and strife,
Now, here in Korea, I long for thee and the day we will together be.

Your loving husband,
Edward

In the autumn of 1951, while I was doing duty in the Korean War, I occasionally observed a flock of swans that inhabited a pond near our campsite. The swans had migrated from Siberia. Watching the swans reminded me of a particular poem from a book of American poems I had been required to study in an English literature class in college. By that time, I had forgotten most of the words of the poem and the name of the author. But, I never forgot the opening words: "Not unlike the swan" and the message conveyed of the swans' love, bonding and mating for life.

On the evening of December 1, 1951, in the quiet of my quarters, reflecting on the message of that poem, and pining for my wife, I penned the following poem to convey my thoughts and feelings for her, I sent this missive with this photo of me enclosed.

From Korea: December 1, 1951

Dear Toussia,

To my wonderful and lovely wife on our fifth wedding anniversary:

Like unto the swan, not held in ransom,
freely willing to take itself and live in the bosom,
of it's love, the lake.

Come sweetheart, in your beautiful stole,
into the bosom of your love, my heart.

Be assimilated into my lonely soul,
and for eternity may we never part.

Your philosophically romanticist and loving husband,

Edward

P.s. Photo enclosed

From Korea: December 8, 1951

Dear Toussia,

Your beautiful portrait arrived yesterday, just in time to remind me of our fifth wedding anniversary and how beautiful you are.

Enclosed you'll find a poem that your portrait inspired.

Your loving husband,
Edward

A Portrait of My Beautiful Wife, Ludmila

On the eve of our fifth wedding anniversary, as I sit here,
in far away Korea, fondly gazing at your beautiful portrait, my dear,
I visualize, not a portrait, but your smiling face so true.
Inevitably, I become terribly lonely, unhappy and very blue.

It seems that you are really sitting before me here.
I know it is but your image, exact, exquisite and clear,
recorded with the patience and genius of a master's painting,
capturing the beams of happiness, that your smile is radiating.

You are very beautiful, lovely, eloquent and oh so warm.
There is no blemish to mar your lovely feminine charm.
On your beautifully smiling and softly dimpled face,
is perpetually expressed true love's heavenly, blissful grace.

Your rosy, blushing cheeks are like ripened apples divinely done,
radiating happiness, like the soft rays of the morning sun.
Your lips are like rubies, so rare and oh so very precious,
and unrivaled in their scarlet magnificence, so glorious.

Your eyes are like diamonds and sapphires inlaid in gold,
sparkling like celestial stars, revealing a happiness to behold.
I also notice those cute, shapely and alert little ears,
always attentive to my wishes, as though always good cheers.

Your luxurious wavy hair, so attractive and beautifully brown,
is like the headdress of a queen, a stately crown.
Your comely little nose accentuates your smile and charms,
and delights my soul with dreams of holding you in my arms.

Your bosom where upon humble modesty does repose,
is the resting place for my weary head, I do suppose.
Everything about you is lovely and fascinating, like a goddess,
created for me alone, to admire and lovingly caress.

I see not a portrait, but your image in an aura of fine artistry,
rich in the beauty of a rainbow, created with an artist's mastery.
There you are, mirrored in the portrait, my love, my paradise,
my dreams come true, Ludmila, my wife, to eternally eulogize.

Though the portrait is an image of your beauty so true,
portraying your loveliness, with happiness always smiling through,
none will compare with the beauty, nor be as clear or stay,
as your image being imprinted on my soul since our wedding day.

PART 10

FLORIDA ASSIGNMENT

EGLIN AIR FORCE BASE, FLORIDA

AFTER 13 MONTHS of a very busy but lonely overseas duty in Korea, I arrived at Travis AFB, California, U.S.A. on March 21, 1952. After such a long separation from my family, it was great to come home to my wonderful wife and three children. The following day we left California by auto, for my next assignment at Eglin AFB, Florida. We vacationed for a month along the way, sightseeing at the Grand Canyon and visiting my folks and relatives in Wood River, Illinois.

May 6, 1952, I reported to Hq. Eglin AF Base (Fort Walton), Florida. I was assigned to Hq. 3202nd Installations Group, as Chief of Group Supply. How do you like that? A bonafide "Staff Supply Officer". On January 20, 1953, I was reassigned a new duty as Chief of Materiel which was even better than just a plain Supply Officer. As Chief of Materiel, I also was in charge of the Supply activities supporting seven auxiliary bases. More prestige--I theenk!--and a heck of a lot more work and responsibility, too.

Eleven months after I returned from Korea, the stork visited us again. Ludmila gave birth to Natalie Ellen, born February 11, 1953, at Eglin AF Base Hospital, Florida. She was named after her Aunt Natalie, Ludmila's only sibling, who was living with us at the time.

In the Spring of 1953, while stationed at Eglin A.F. Base, Fort Walton, Florida, we visited my parents in Wood River, Illinois. We took our four daughters and their Aunt Natalie with us in our station wagon. Natalie and Eugene were still living with us. Eugene was stepfather to Ludmila and Natalie, they called him "Papa Pye"—translated it is "daddy nice". Our children thought they were saying "Popeye", which they made his new nickname.

During that visit to Wood River, Natalie met my youngest brother Arthur Joseph (who went by both "Joe" and "Art" due to mix-up on his birth certificate). Joe took a liking to Natalie immediately.

In the above photo is our newly expanded family. Ludmila is holding our newest addition, Natalie Ellen, born February 11, 1953. Her big sisters (right to left) Ann, Mary and Irene, were now 6, 4, and 3 years of age, respectively. Ludmila's only sister, Natalie Ellen's namesake, is on the left.

Our children's Aunt Natalie and Uncle Joe dated during that first visit and afterward corresponded frequently. By November 21, 1953, having fallen in love in a whirlwind romance, the two were married at Eglin A.F. Base, and Eugene gave away the bride.

Joe, known by our children as "Uncle Art", and their
Aunt Natalie, are pictured here on their wedding day,
November 21, 1953 at Eglin A.F. Base, Florida.
Eugene is visible in the background on the left side
of the photo. Since we two Trautt brothers married
two sisters, all our children have the exact same
grandparents.

Shortly after their wedding, Joe and Natalie moved to
Sacramento where they raised 5 children, Joseph, Jr.,
Catherine, Lydia, Mary, and Michael. They remained in the
Sacramento area for their entire careers.

When first married, Joe attended Sacramento State College
under the Veterans G.I. Bill and was working part time as an
insurance salesman. After college, he was employed as a
photographer at Aerojet General Corporation in Sacramento
for seven years, before accepting a job with the California

Youth Authority. He left that job for health reasons after 15 years. From then on, he worked in entrepreneurial sales until he retired in 1999.

Natalie was a supermom, she was a homemaker for the first 14 years of their marriage. Then, in 1967, she was hired by the U.S. Postal Service in Sacramento. She worked for the Postal Service for 32 years before she retired in 1999, the same year as Joe.

CAREER AND FAMILY EVENTS

IN TERMS OF MY MILITARY CAREER, 1954 was a very good year, having received a promotion to Lt. Colonel in May. But, the rest of the year was very difficult emotionally, because my mother was hospitalized that summer for a gall bladder operation and soon afterward my dad was hospitalized. Dad didn't recover and passed away on September 12, 1954. I was grateful that I had the opportunity to visit with my father not long before his death. It was an unexpected loss for me and my brothers and sisters, and we worried about how our mother would do, since she was in poor health and depended so much on our father.

For me, it took several months for reality to set in. Since I had a family of my own and because we lived about 700 miles from my parents' home, it seemed that my dad was still with us. Then about six months later, when we visited my mother, I realized that dad was indeed gone, on to his eternal reward, and I was never to enjoy his presence again in this life.

Reality hit me like a ton of bricks. I had to accept the fact that my mom was now alone, in her empty home, facing the reality of the loss of his presence, especially his love and helping hand. My siblings and I all agreed to visit mom as often as possible. We did so until God called her home to the paradise in the kingdom of God, reunited with her husband for eternity.

This photo of me on the left, with my mother seated, was taken with my siblings when we gathered for dad's funeral. Left to right behind me are Stephen, John, Margaret, Cyril, Lyle and Norbert. John's 2 year old daughter Debbie is standing next to my mom.

A year after my promotion to Lt. Colonel on May 10, 1954, and eight months after my dad died, Ludmila gave birth to our first son. He is our fifth child, and was born May 9, 1955, at Eglin A.F. Base Hospital. We named him John Edward after my father and me.

Our 5th child, John Edward.

On July 18, 1955, I was reassigned from Eglin AF Base, Florida, and directed to report to Fort Hamilton, Brooklyn, New York, not later than September 20, 1955, with my wife and five children, for air transport to my new assignment in Bitburg, Germany.

We decided that with five children in tow, it was time for "Popeye", Ludmila's stepfather, to move into separate living quarters. He was very sad to see us go, and our children missed him, too. We found a senior living residence with other Russian residents in San Francisco, where he remained for the rest of his life until he passed away 4 years later.

We left Florida driving to New York in our 8-passenger 1953 Chevy station wagon. En route, we visited my still grieving mother and other relatives for a couple of weeks in Mascoutah, Illinois. On September 23, 1955, we flew from New York to Rhein-Main AF Base, Germany, then by rail to my next assignment at Bitburg, Germany. The station wagon followed us to Germany by ship transport.

PART 11

GERMANY ASSIGNMENT

BITBURG, GERMANY

ON SEPTEMBER 28, 1955, I was assigned to Hq. 36th Air Base Group as Commander of the 36th Supply Squadron, Bitburg, Germany. I enjoyed that command assignment very much, and the family enjoyed Germany. But Ludmila with 5 small children had her hands full, even with a full-time maid to help. Our family grew exponentially with the next pregnancy, when on August 20, 1956, Ludmila gave birth to twins.

Pictured above are our twins, Thomas Alan Trautt (left) and Teresa Alice Trautt (right). They were born at the Bitburg AF Base Hospital on August 20, 1956. When asked who was born first, Ludmila, would with smile say that Tom was a gentleman, 'ladies first.' Teresa arrived about 5 minutes before Tom.

January 15, 1957, I was reassigned as Base Assistant Director of Materiel at Bitburg AFB. The following month, I was reassigned as Base Director of Materiel--going up the (Supply-Aircraft Maintenance) career ladder. My assigned duty was Chief, or boss, if you prefer, of all the base aircraft maintenance and supply functions. That was a new experience with increased authority and awesome responsibility. I fully enjoyed that duty for the next 18 months—when I received my reassignment back to the U.S.A.

This is our 1957 Christmas family photo, our children, left to right, seated are Teresa, John, Natalie, Tom, and standing are Mary, Ann, Irene.

On July 1, 1958, three years after we arrived in Germany, I was reassigned from Bitburg AF Base, Germany to Harlingen AF Base, Texas and directed to report to Rhein-Main AFB, with my family (now seven kids--five girls and two boys aged about two through eleven) for air transport to U.S.A., Ft. Hamilton, Brooklyn, N.Y. We picked up our green Chevy station wagon at the Brooklyn port and then drove from New York to Harlingen AF Base, Texas. En route to my assignment in Texas, we visited my mother and other relatives in Wood River, Illinois.

PART 12

TEXAS ASSIGNMENT

ASSIGNMENT ENDS IN BASE CLOSURE
Harlingen Air Force Base, Texas

We arrived at our destination, Hq. 3610 Navigator Training Wing (Air Training Command), Harlingen Air Force Base, Texas, on August 29, 1958. I was assigned the duty of Base Supply Officer, a $40 million account. At this point in my military career, I was very happy with my supply assignments and enjoying the new challenges. Not long after we arrived, we bought a three bedroom, two bath house with a carport located at 925 Grimes Street.

Our four school aged children were enrolled in a nearby Catholic School, which was within walking distance. In good weather, they would all caravan on bicycles to school en masse along with neighbors, including a boy named "Butch", who was their designated leader when Ann wasn't present. It rained a lot that year in Harlingen and the children loved playing in the flooded yards and streets.

Ludmila discovered a fabulous pancake restaurant, which we frequented on Sunday mornings after church. Often, after brunch, we would all change into swimsuits and pile into the Green Chevy for a trip to Padre Island and a day in the sun on the beach. Those were very good and happy years.

My mother's health had been steadily declining after my father died. And in the early spring of 1959, it worsened to the point that it was difficult to manage on her own. We discussed the situation with my brothers and sisters and made the decision to bring her to live with us. In the summer of 1959, when she was 74 years old, grandma moved in with us.

Our 8th child, Catherine Gail, was born at Baptist Hospital, Harlingen, Texas on February 4, 1960, which, coincidentally, is her mother's birthday, too.

Grandma, happily holding Catherine Gail,
our seventh child.

On February 11, 1960, The week after Cathy was born, I received the "Commendatory Achievement Award" from Department of Air Force, Pentagon, Washington, D.C., for "Outstanding Performance of Supply Officer Duties." Later that year, on July 20, I was reassigned as Wing Hq. Director of Materiel– that's chief (commander) of all base aircraft maintenance and supply functions. Hey, that was quite a new management experience, with more authority and responsibility than any previous assignments.

With my new position, and higher salary, and bursting at the seams in our 3 bedroom house, we started looking in earnest for a larger home. We found and purchased a much bigger home on Washington Street in Harlingen. It was a 4 bedroom home with a large living room in the front, a family room and dining room and a 2 car garage in the rear. The kids loved the spacious new house even better than the house that we vacated on Grimes Street.

The following year, on March 23, 1961, I received a second "Outstanding Supply Officer's Award," from Department of Air Force, Pentagon, Washington, D.C. That award, in recognition of my accomplishments in supply management, was very much appreciated. At that point in time, I realized that I had made the right decision, when a few years before, I requested that my career specialty be changed from Food Service to Staff Supply and/or command duties.

This was a typical Sunday morning in our house in 1961, ready for church. Left to right are Natalie, Irene, Grandma Trautt, Mary, Tom, John, and Ludmila holding Catherine

By late 1961, the political climate in Washington, D.C. had changed and on March 30, 1961 it was announced that the Base with its 245 buildings would be closed and phased out by the end of 1962. From a city with a population of 13,235 in 1941 before the first military installation was opened, to a population of 41,000 by 1960, the base closure severely impacted Harlingen.

The sale of 1,400 houses in 1963 due to the base closure

(including ours) depressed the real estate market in Harlingen for years to follow. We were forced to sell our house at a significant loss. During that last year in Harlingen, before the base closed (after we sold our new house) we moved into a five bedroom family housing unit on the Base, which had been converted from troop barracks.

It was there that our ninth child, Elizabeth Agnes, was born at Baptist Hospital, Harlingen, Texas. Elizabeth was a "blue baby" (Rh factor) and required an emergency blood exchange at birth. She needed special comforting when she was taken home. We were fortunate to have my mother living with us at the time. Much of the needed extra attention was provided by grandma who loved to rock her

Ludmila holding Elizabeth in the foreground, with big sisters
(left to right) Irene, Mary and Natalie.

Grandma always had her own room when she lived with us. She spent a lot of time with the babies and was very attached to them. The older children remember spending many hours listening to her stories, sometimes the same story more often than once. They all have fond memories of her from the years she spent with us.

LAUGHLIN AIR FORCE BASE, TEXAS

ON MARCH 15, 1962, I was promoted to Colonel--my reward for managing my assignments as best I could, with on-the-job learning experiences, good horse-sense, knowledge, diligence and grit. On May 10th, I was reassigned as Commander of the Aircraft Maintenance and Supply Group (M&S Gp.) at Laughlin AF Base, Del Rio, Texas.

Official promotion photo, Colonel, US Air Force, 1962.

Brigadier General Pechals, Director of Materiel (Hq. Air Training Command, San Antonio, Texas, selected me for the assignment and told me that my assignments as M&S Gp. Commander at Harlingen and Laughlin were exceptional and that it was extremely rare for a non-flying officer in the Air Training Command to be assigned duty as Commander of a Maintenance and Supply Group.

I surmise that my accomplishments in aircraft mechanics school, the management of supply functions and as squadron commander for several years had been recognized and resulted in those assignments as group commander.

In May, 1962, after being stationed four years at Harlingen AF Base, Texas, we drove to my new assignment at Headquarters 3646 Pilot Training Wing (Air Training Command), Laughlin AF Base, Del Rio, Texas. We traveled in our two station wagons, the old green 1953 Chevy and a new light blue, 1962 Plymouth with rear fender fins. In addition to Ludmila and I, we had a total of nine children to transport (seven girls and two boys, aged almost one to almost fifteen) plus my mother, "Gamma".

On May 13, 1962, I reported for duty as Commander, 3646th Maintenance and Supply Group, Laughlin AFB, Del Rio, Texas. The Laughlin M.&S. Group was composed of Group Hq. Squadron, three Aircraft Maintenance Squadrons, and a Supply Squadron with over 3,000 personnel (including military and civilian employees).

On July 20, 1962, I was awarded the Air Force Commendation Medal. My commanding officer stated that the award was, "for outstanding managerial service as Base Supply Officer and Commander of the 3610 Maintenance and Supply Group, Harlingen, Texas, for the period of September 5, 1958, to June 18, 1962." It sure is a wonderful feeling when your boss, the General, recognizes your abilities and accomplishments and affirms such in writing.

One year later, on May 6, 1963, I reported to Chanute AFB, Rantoul, Illinois to attend "Materiel Management for Commanders and Staff Officers." The course was designed for officers of the rank of Colonel and General with staff or command assignments in Supply, Aircraft Maintenance, or Materiel. I graduated from the course and returned to Laughlin AFB with my brain stuffed full of command and leadership theories and some good, practical, down-to-earth, tried and tested, common horse-sense management concepts.

It was very gratifying and encouraging to me, this late in my military career, to find out that the management and/or command skills which I developed by a sort of self initiated (learn as you go), hands-on approach, were pretty much the accepted norm or rule-of-thumb for the course. I came away from that management course feeling pretty proud of myself. It was a long, winding and bumpy road from that little family farm in Akron, Iowa, to that military training course for top level military materiel officers.

On July 15, 1963, I was reassigned as Wing Deputy Commander for Materiel. Nothing had really changed, I was still Commander of the aircraft maintenance and supply functions on the base, it was the same job as before, just a new, fancy title.

May 17, 1964, was the dawn of a new era in pilot training at Laughlin AF Base, Del Rio, Texas. The base now had the T-38A Talon aircraft--the latest "New Look" USAF twin-engine jet, supersonic pilot trainer aircraft. My M&S Gp. troops performed the maintenance and supply services for the new aircraft.

The knowledge I gained from the Aircraft Mechanics School at Keesler Field, Mississippi in 1941 and the several years of staff and command supply duties prepared me well for the new tasks at hand. I enjoyed that assignment of Wing Deputy Commander right up to the time of my retirement from the Air Force.

In 1965, our four bedroom house was again too small for our needs. Grandma was still living with us, our tenth child was on the way and our two boys had reached an age where privacy was an important issue. Also, grandma's health needs were increasing and the doctor informed us she would soon be unable to travel. So, we made arrangements to take grandma back to Illinois to live with my brother Norbert, who was living alone at the time.

My mother had lived with us for five and a half years and it was difficult for all of us to say goodbye. For the next few years, Norbert provided her with the personal loving care and attention she needed and deserved until she became severely ill in 1967 and entered an Alton, Illinois hospital, where she died at the age of 81.

In February, 1967, I joined my siblings in Alton, Illinois, to attend our mother's funeral. Pictured from left to right, standing are John, Catherine, Edward, Robert, Stephen, Joseph. Seated in front are Margaret and Norbert.

On October 29, 1965, Antoinette (Toni) Frances, our 10th, and last child was born on my mother's birthday at the Laughlin AF Base hospital in Del Rio, Texas (grand total eight girls, two boys). Like Elizabeth, Toni was at risk at birth due to her Rh blood factor. The doctors performed a Caesarean section delivery (one month premature), which was followed immediately with a blood exchange. With the addition of Toni, all twelve seats at our dining room table were now occupied. It was time to inform the stork to delete our address from future deliveries.

Photo of Ludmila with our last child, Antoinette Frances in her arms and flanked by the other two youngest children, Cathy on the left and Elizabeth on the right.

Betsy Robinson, wrote an article for the "Low Jet" Laughlin Air Force Base monthly publication, in June, 1966, that described meeting Ludmila in the obstetrician's office while she was waiting for her appointment for her first pregnancy. The article was a full page long, and described our busy household charmingly.

Ms. Robinson said about Ludmila, "I couldn't help but notice the calm, relaxed woman who sat down next to me. Her sweet smile and contented look made me think that this must also be her first child, so I said something to that effect. Her smile broadened and her eyes twinkled as she replied, 'No, not the first, this is the tenth.' Toussia Trautt is proud of every one of her family for you can hear it in her voice as she talks lovingly of each one "

Celebrating Ludmila's 44th birthday in 1966, Ann's soon to be husband Mark Rymsza is seated with her and Ludmila is holding Toni.

Left to right seated are Cathy and Elizabeth. Standing in the back are Irene, Mary, John, barely visible Tom, and Teresa. The only sibling not visible in this photo is Natalie.

In April, 1966, the Air Force Personnel Office informed me of my retirement date, scheduled for November 1, 1966. I was also informed that I was required to have a retirement physical exam at Lackland AF Base Hospital, San Antonio, Texas, at least 60 days before my retirement date. In July, 1966, while I stayed in San Antonio for my physical, my family (now 10 kids aged eight mos. to 18 years) moved to Sacramento. My brother J.P. ("Uncle Art" to the kids) drove one station wagon and 18 year old daughter Ann and 15 year old Irene took turns driving the other station wagon. They drove from Del Rio, Texas to Sacramento, California in two days. They stopped at a motel in Tucson, Arizona for a needed and welcome rest, and also to visit my father's brother, Uncle Frank Trautt, and his family who were living in Tucson.

We moved our family into a rental property for a short time until we were able to close escrow on a modest tract home on Cathay Way, in Sacramento, one block from El Camino High School, and within walking distance for our children.

Our oldest child, Ann, was married to Mark Rymsza on August 27, 1966, at Mather AF Base Chapel, Sacramento, California. I drove from Del Rio to Sacramento for the wedding in our oldest of three cars, a 1953 green Chevy station wagon with three bench seats (our older children had unaffectionately dubbed it the "green monster").

I still had another two months of service remaining until my retirement, so, a few days after the wedding, I flew back to Lackland by military aircraft, leaving my family to settle in for the start of school. After my retirement ceremony, two months later, on November 1, 1966, I flew back to Sacramento to join my wife and children who were patiently awaiting my return.

PART 13

MILITARY EVENTS

WORLD WIDE MILITARY ASSIGNMENTS

MY WORLD WIDE MILITARY DUTY assignments took me to all of the continents of the world except Australia and Antarctica. In the America's my assignments took me to Mexico, Brazil, Canada and almost all the states in the U.S., including Hawaii and Alaska. In overseas service, I traveled to many different countries in Europe, North Africa, the Middle East and the Far East including the following, respectively:

France, Germany, Holland, Belgium, Luxemburg, Portugal, Spain, Austria, Switzerland, Italy, Greece

Algiers, Libya, Morocco, Tunisia, Liberia

India, Nepal, Pakistan, Burma, Kashmir, Arabia, Iran

China, Korea, Japan, Siam (now Thailand), Malaya, Vietnam

In fact, those Air Force travels took me to some of the world's largest cities such as Paris, Vienna, Bonn, Rome, Tripoli, Athens, Delhi, Bombay, Calcutta, Rangoon, Mandalay, Singapore, Bangkok, Saigon, Kunming, Seoul, Tokyo and many others too numerous to mention.

During those military travels, I took advantage of vacation time that I had accumulated and any spare time I could arrange to visit and enjoy many of the world's natural scenic wonders, man-made structures and places or monuments of historical significance. In addition to the sightseeing, I was also interested in observing how the cultures and religious customs differed in the many countries I visited. Without a doubt, my vacation time was enjoyable and educational. Some of my most memorable sightseeing excursions are listed below:

U.S.A.-- Niagara Falls, Glacier National Park, Yellowstone National Park, the Grand Canyon, the Metropolitan Museum of Art

Paris, France-- Eiffel Tower, Louvre Museum and other historical attractions

Rome, Italy-- St. Peters Cathedral, the Vatican, 27 B.C. Pantheon, the Colosseum Amphitheater, the catacombs and many ancient ruins

Athens, Greece-- Parthenon Temple, Acropolis ruins and other historical structures

Agra, India-- Taj Mahal and ancient ruins and temples in other parts of India

Bangkok, Siam-- Temple of the Emerald Buddha, the King's Palace and scenic wonders

Kunming, China-- Marco Polo Road (China to Burma Road on to Ledo Road in India), and other historical attractions

During my military overseas service, I also took time to socialize with the local citizens. I always found myself treated as a privileged military guest. On several occasions, I was invited to their homes to share their indigenous meals, an honor I always heartily enjoyed and appreciated.

MILITARY CAMPAIGNS
Participation by Edward Trautt

World War II Campaigns		
National Defense Service Medal w/1 Battle Star	12/7/1941 to 1/28/1946	WDAGO 1/28/1946
Asiatic Pacific Campaign Medal w/3 Battle Stars		
India-Burma	4/2/1942 to 1/28/1945	WDAGO 2/1/1946
Asiatic Pacific	4/20/1942 to 1/28/1946	WDAGO 2/1/1946
China Offensive	5/5/1945 to 9/2/1945	WDAGO 1/1/1946

Korean Campaigns		
Korean Campaigns-Authority AFP-900-12 Korean Service Medal w/4 Battle Stars		
First United Nations Counter Offensive	1/25/1951 to 4/21/1951	GO 78 FEAF 1952
Chinese Communist Forces Spring Offensive	4/22/1951 to 7/8/1951	GO 78 FEAF 1952
United Nations Summer-Fall	7/9/1951 to 11/27/1952	GO 500 FEAF 10/30/1952
Second Korean Winter	11/28/1951 to 4/30/1952	GO 500 FEAF 10/30/1952

Reference:

AFP	Air Force Personnel
FEAF	Far Eastern Air Force
GO	General Order
ICD-ATC	India-China Division, Air Transport Command
WDAGO	War Department Adjutant General's Office .

MEDALS AND RIBBONS

Ribbons awarded to Edward Trautt
for service from June 30, 1940 to November 1, 1996

Ribbons are shown above as worn by Edward on his USAF dress uniform. The corresponding names of each of ribbons are listed below in the same order.

Top Row	Army Commendation Medal	Air Force Commendation Medal	Air Force Outstanding Unit Award Ribbon
Row 2	American Defense Service Medal	American Campaign Medal	Asiatic Pacific Campaign Medal w/ 3 Battle Stars
Row 3	European-African-Middle Eastern Campaign Medal	World War II Victory Medal	National Defense Service Medal w/ 1 Battle Star
Row 4	Korean Service Campaign Medal w/ 4 Battle Stars	Air Force Longevity Service Award Ribbon w/ Bronze Oak Leaf Cluster	United Nations Service Medal
Row 5	Republic of Korea Presidential Unit Citation Ribbon	China War Memorial Medal	Korean War Service Medal

RETIREMENT CEREMONY

THE U.S. ARMED FORCES underwent major restructuring during the WWII period due to its increased size and complexity of operations. I had enlisted in 1940 with the Wisconsin National Guard Artillery, and ordered to active Federal duty in the U.S. Army within 4 months of enlistment. My original intent was to serve only for the duration of the impending war, which I had expected to be short lived, but that was not to be. After my first year of active military duty, I reenlisted in the U.S. Army Air Corps and 3 months later, on March 9, 1942, the" U.S. Army Air Corps" became the "U.S. Army Air Forces". Later, on September 18, 1947, the U.S. Army Air Forces were detached from the U.S. Army and became the US Air Force (USAF), equal in status with the Army & Navy, and which I served in until my military retirement.

In serving my country in her call to arms, I joined with my American comrades in arms, who were just plain ordinary folks like me, who loved their country. We all responded to her call, as Americans always will, when our peace and freedom and all that we stand for in this great democracy is threatened. We, the citizen soldiers of WWII, 16,600,000 of us, were well organized and disciplined, and intent on stopping the tyranny that we fought against. We came from every walk of life and from every corner of this great and proud democratic nation to answer our nation's call to arms.

Shortly after college graduation, I enlisted in the Army as a Private. My first assignment was company cook, serving meals to 350 troops. I served for 26 years of active military duty, seven of which were overseas. My last duty assignment was commander of an Aircraft Maintenance-Supply Group with about 3,000 personnel. I was proud to serve.

I was formally retired as a Colonel from the U.S. Air Force, on November 1, 1966, at Lackland AF Base, San Antonio, Texas. During the retirement ceremony, my thoughts turned to the eloquent words I had heard from General Douglas MacArthur in his retirement address before Congress on April 19, 1951, after being relieved of all of his commands in Korea-Japan by President Harry S. Truman, "Old Soldiers never die, they just fade away." I remember that speech by General MacArthur and another he delivered at the U.S. Military Academy at West Point on May 12, 1962, about "Duty, Honor, Country." In my mind, those two addresses were the best and most inspiring that I was privileged to hear during my military career.

Retirement ceremony, November 1, 1966.
Certificate of Retirement presented by
Brigadier General Frank P. Wood at Hq. Air Training Command,
Lackland Air Force Base, San Antonio, Texas

I departed by military aircraft from Kelly AF Base, San Antonio, Texas to Mather AF Base, Sacramento, California, where my wonderful wife, Ludmila, and our large family, were patiently waiting for me to join them in our new "first retirement" home on Cathay Way.

In telling the story of my military service, I intentionally refrained from writing about the terrible human suffering and death and the destruction of property that I witnessed. Like most of us survivors of war, we seldom speak of such things. I leave that to the documentarians, historians, and war correspondents. Nonetheless, I am often tortured by visions of the sacrifices endured by my comrades, many of them gave their lives defending freedom and justice. War deprived them of "life, liberty and the pursuit of happiness". They were robbed of their futures, and the opportunity to write their life's story. Also, their families and friends were deprived of the privilege of experiencing what would or could have been. War is a human tragedy.

PART 14

POST MILITARY

CIVIL SERVICE

AFTER RETIRING from the military November 1, 1966, it took only a few days until I became preoccupied with the "what do I do now" syndrome. Just as many retirees before me, I simply planned to take it easy and relax. But relax, I didn't. I became more bored and frustrated, especially each morning when almost every other adult male in the neighborhood was off to some kind of job. I started quietly inquiring about jobs. I found very few likely prospects. Oh yes, there were jobs of all kinds advertised in all the newspapers--but--who wants or needs to go from house to house, peddling encyclopedias, vacuum cleaners, cosmetics, magazine subscriptions, etc.? That's when I decided that there were lots of jobs worse than teaching school.

Having a Bachelor of Science degree from Superior State Teacher's College (now University of Wisconsin) at Superior and a Wisconsin Teaching Credential, I decided to contact the California State Office of Superintendent of Schools in Sacramento about teaching requirements. That got me started in the right place. I applied for and received a temporary California Teaching Credential which qualified me for "substitute teaching" in California schools.

Two days later, I received my first call to substitute teach a class in biology. That day and many more that followed, went great. I enjoyed teaching biology and chemistry for almost two years, from January, 1967 through October, 1968. In August, 1968, I had applied for a job as a Sanitarian for the Yolo County Health Department and was hired for the position, starting November, 1968. In 1970, I was promoted to

Occupational Health Sanitarian and served in that position until I retired in May, 1980, at age 65.

When I retired from the Air Force in 1966, my family had already relocated to California and I was staying temporarily alone in San Antonio. This time, my retirement celebration was much more memorable. All of our 10 children and their young families attended (10 grandchildren--Guy, Glenn, and Joy (Rymsza), Christy, Sandi, and Helen (Anderson), Liz, Lenny, Eddie, and new-born Ricky (Montenegro), plus two on the way—Maynard Bernavage and Katie Anderson). Also, about 200 local business people and county employees joined in the celebration.

My 2nd retirement, was a mini-family reunion, with all of our 10 children in attendance, standing from left to right are Ann, Toni, Irene, Mary, Natalie, Cathy and Teresa. Seated are Elizabeth and Tom (left) , John (right).

Newspaper clipping for my second retirement:

MONDAY, APRIL 28, 1980   THE DAVIS ENTERPRISE, DAVIS, CALIF.   PAGE 3

Second time's a charm

WOODLAND — One retirement party isn't enough for some people, not when they've had two careers.

Edward Trautt retired as a full colonel from the U.S. Air Force in 1966. He celebrated again Sunday, when some 200 people were on hand at Ed and Toussia Trautt's 110 College St. residence in honor of his retirement after 11½ years as occupational health sanitarian with the Yolo County Health Department.

The Trautts have 10 children, all of whom joined their father for his second retirement party. His daughters, Irene Anderson and Toni Trautt, and his son, Tom Trautt, live in Davis.

John, Teresa, Cathy and Lisa Trautt are Woodland residents. Coming in for the event are his children, Ann Rymsza of Chicago, Mary Bernavage of South Carolina and Natalie Montenegro of Los Angeles.

The occasion marks the first time the Trautt offspring have been able to be together in 10 years, making it a family reunion, along with the Trautts' seven grandchildren.

In 1969, the Trautts moved into a home built in 1893, formerly Woodland's first hospital. They hope to settle in Davis following his retirement.

His daughter, Irene Anderson, characterizes her father as "part of an old breed who sincerely believes in the concept of providing a service to people and being positive,

Ed Trautt and his wife, Toussia, celebrate his second retirement at a combination retirement party and

family reunion at the Trautt home Sunday.

Enterprise photo

not negative, in providing assistance to people with their plans and problems."

He was a substitute science teacher in Sacramento schools in 1967.

Trautt's community activities include his three-year chairmanship of the

Bilingual Committee for Beamer School (he also assisted in the development of the program); participation in the Knights of Columbus; board membership in the Yolo County Economic Opportunity Committee; participation in activities

of the Davis Newman Center.

Trautt's many friends throughout the county include people in the food industry, housing and home-planning fields and those in environmental health.

247

ENJOYING RETIREMENT

AFTER MY SECOND RETIREMENT in 1980, I finally found time to relax and enjoy life, I planted large vegetable and flower gardens in the back yard. In the cool of the evening breezes, I shared the beautiful golden sunsets with my wife, buddy and life-time companion, Ludmila.

In 1981, Ludmila and I traveled by airplane to France. In Paris, we visited her former school friends. In Rouen (Normandy), France, we visited her Aunt Tanya. In Dax, southern France, we stayed with her cousin Elizabeth (Perebaskine) and her husband, Dr. Jean Raynaud.

In the spring of 1982, Ludmila and I, took a four month trip by auto to the four corners of the U.S.A., with a side trip to Mexico and Canada, visiting old military friends and relatives on several stops along the way. While vacationing in Texas, we received word about the death of Ludmila's Aunt Tanya.

In late summer, 1983, we vacationed on the Oregon and California coastline of the Pacific Ocean. In October, I had a mild heart attack and was hospitalized for one week. A followup medical exam in March, 1984 indicated all was well and I was back to reasonably good health. So, a few months later, we went to Europe by airplane to again visit Ludmila's remaining relatives and friends.

By this time, our 100 year old, 10 room house at 110 College Street, Woodland, California, was too big and too old for us. Our daughter Irene was then a realtor and helped us find a wonderful, modern, two-bedroom home in the Village Homes Planned Development in Davis, California. At the time the project was a new experimental, nationally acclaimed, solar-oriented, semi-communal subdivision, and we moved into our much smaller home at 2508 Overhill Lane in April, 1986.

For all families, there are happy and joyful times and there are also times of sadness and tears. About a year after I retired, tragedy struck home. Our grandchild, Christina, who had been diagnosed with Leukemia six years earlier, at the age of 3, died from an overdose of cancer treatment on July 3, 1981. I have so many fond memories of Christina, as a baby, a toddler and growing into an affectionate, always smiling, beautiful girl. I remember her best for the times when she asked me to hold her and sing to her. Whenever she found me relaxing in our famous old oak rocking chair, she would jump onto my lap and say, "I like you, Grandpa." She would usually fall asleep in my arms as I rocked her and sang to her. When she awoke or decided to get down, she would always say, "You are nice, Grandpa, I love you." Christina was born September 4, 1972, and on July 3, 1981, she entered paradise in the Kingdom of God.

Indeed, little girls are sweet and nice, like sugar and spice. There is no innocence like that of a little child–always so honest and trusting of those nearest and dearest to them. To be sure, we should never give them cause to doubt that gentleness, trust and faith they place in us.

Tragedy continues to strike as the years pass. We have since lost one of our daughters and a son in law. In June 2010, our beautiful, intelligent, talented and witty daughter Natalie Montenegro succumbed to cancer. She was 57 years old. Her sense of humor sustained her during her long illness. The following year, Martin Bernavage, our daughter Mary's husband, also died from cancer. Marty was 59 years old, he was my comrade-in-arms. We were both active members of American Legion Post 77, Woodland, California, in the last several years preceding his illness and death.

TIME MARCHES ON

BY THIS TIME TOMORROW, today's events will be yesterday's memories, and tomorrow will be today and everyone alive will be one day older. Today will have receded into the past of one day, then a week, a month and eventually one year and on and on into eternity. So, on we go today, creating what will be our yesterday's and yesteryear's memories. We often take today for granted, and old age slowly sneaks up on you, if you are lucky.

The year of 1992 was just another year that sped by while we relaxed in the slow lane of life. In 1993, we had our last extended vacation, traveling along the California coast from San Francisco to San Diego, enjoying the beach and dining out. Along the way, we visited with our son Tom in Santa Barbara, our son John and his family in Long Beach, our nephew Michael Trautt in San Diego and some of our friends in southern California. Oh, what fun we had visiting everyone, and how wonderful it was taking many strolls along the ocean beach with my special pal and sweetheart, Ludmila.

In the spring of 1994, I became aware of a pronounced ringing and hearing loss in my left ear, as well as an occasional episode of dizziness. During World War II, while stationed in India, I had made numerous flights in non-pressurized aircraft over the Himalaya Mountains (the Hump), at altitudes up to 30,000 feet above sea level. Apparently, the high altitudes caused damage to my inner ear.

Ludmila has had a long history of poor hearing, and now, compounded with my hearing loss, our conversations are sometimes a bit confusing. They can go something like this:

"Today it's windy."
"Are you sure it's Wednesday?"
"No, it's Thursday."
"Yes, I'm thirsty, too."
"What were you saying?"
"Did you say something?"
"I can't find my earring."
"My hearing isn't too good either."

Growing old just seems to be one darned thing after another. In May of 1994, at age 79, I noticed I was having chest pains whenever I walked at a fast pace. My doctor ordered an angiogram which revealed that some of my heart arteries were severely clogged. Two days later, June 6, 1994, I underwent heart surgery with a quadruple bypass. That was 18 years ago, I am one of the lucky ones.

After I recovered sufficiently from my by-pass surgery, Ludmila and I visited our daughter Elizabeth and her family in Ogden, Utah. The cool mountain air and a snow storm brought a new vitality, and I began working on these memoirs in earnest once again.

And now, as I conclude this writing, in 2012, I am 97 and Ludmila is 90. We both still walk, talk, and drive our buick. We have been very fortunate.

To what do I attribute our longevity? – good genes, good medical, good food, (especially home-made chicken soup), moderation in drink and exercise, and last, but not least, a lovable and loving family.

STILL SERVNG

AT AGE 97, I am still enjoying my life membership in the Knights of Columbus, have served one term as Grand Knight and a couple of other officer positions.

I am a life-time member of the "Veterans of Foreign Wars," Post 6949, Davis, California, and have served as Post Chaplain. I am also a life member of the American Legion Post 77, Woodland, California. I have served as 2nd Vice Commander, 1st Vice Commander and in 2009, elected Post Commander. During my term as commander, at age 95, I was honored for being the oldest American Legion Post Commander in the United States.

Since 2007, I have been very busy on behalf of the American Legion and VFW, giving speeches for memorial ceremonies, for high school and college graduation programs, and participating in local civic activities. I am blessed to have had the opportunity to give back to our service men and women and our community in this small way.

May 2009, giving a speech at American Legion Memorial Day Ceremonies,

PART 15

CONCLUSION

FATE

AS I LOOK BACK on my growing up years, as well as the many years of military service, I remember my life as happy and eventful. This is not to say that nothing unhappy or distressful ever happened to me, but simply, that I prefer to dwell on the good things in life. In fact, when I do think about some of the exciting moments in my life, I now realize that some of the events were fraught with danger. Listed below are a few examples of the close encounters and near misses that I sustained as I traveled down life's highway:

- Preschool bear hunting trip.
- A case of the "Spanish" flu influenza at age 4, in 1918 which worldwide claimed the lives of between 50 and 100 million people, including my brother Vincent who was 7 years old. The Spanish flu was one of the deadliest natural disasters in human history.
- A near-drowning incident at age 12.
- An auto accident at age 18, the auto was destroyed, but neither the driver nor my brother Cyril or I were seriously injured.
- An airplane crash at age 28 which resulted in my hospitalization for one month in an Army hospital and another month of recuperation before I returned to military duty.
- On January 4, 1944, after delivering me and 54 Air Force personnel from Florida to Karachi, India, the airplane crashed on its next landing, killing all aboard.

• When stationed in Calcutta, India, Japanese ground fire hit the airplane I was traveling in during its approach for landing at Myitkyina Air Force Base, Burma, January, 1945.

• Caught in unbelievable air turbulence during a flight over the Himalaya Mountains, August, 1945.

• I missed an airplane flight from Calcutta, India to Paris, France, in February, 1946, due to a delay in processing my orders which put me on the next flight out. The plane that I missed crashed into the Adriatic Sea on its approach to the airport in Rome, Italy, killing all but 10 of the 55 on board.

• At Orly Field, Paris, France, in October, 1946, I was already boarding the aircraft when Headquarters called me back to work on a priority project for the General. That plane crashed in the Alps shortly after takeoff, killing all aboard.

• In 1951, while traveling by jeep in a military convoy from Taegu to Pusan in Korea, we were hurrying to get back to the base before dark. Only a few miles from the base, we were caught in sniper cross fire, the jeep following mine closely was hit and all four soldiers in that jeep were killed.

•While traveling from Pusan to Seoul, Korea by overnight train in 1951, about 3:00 A.M., a few miles from Seoul, the train was attacked by hit-and-run snipers using 20 mm guns. The engine and all train cars of the moving train were hit. One person was reported killed and about a dozen were injured. The car that I was in was hit by several bullets but no one was seriously injured, just shaken up a bit from the shower of flying glass and debris.

FULL MEASURE OF LIFE

I HEARD, OR READ SOMEWHERE, that no man has tasted the full measure of life, until he has experienced poverty, war and love.

When I was young, I lived through the poverty of the Great Depression of 1929. During the 1940's, I served in WWII, in the 1950's I served in the Korean War.

While stationed in Paris, France, in July 1946, I was introduced to the love of my life, Ludmila Perebaskine, who I married six months later.

Now, December 2011, having been married to Ludmila for 65 years, we both can proclaim that Divine Providence has smiled kindly upon both of us — giving us ten wonderful, loving and generous children, thirty grandchildren and 15 great grand children to date.

Yes, indeed, I am happy and proud to state that I have truly experienced a "Full Measure of Life."

A LONG AND HAPPY LIFE

TO BE SURE, I have enjoyed a long and happy life, with negligible adversity. My life spanned 85 years of the 20th century and a dozen years, so far, into the 21st. Except for the wars during my lifetime which resulted in considerable human suffering, death and destruction of property, I consider myself fortunate to have lived in what I believe to be the greatest of all times. Indeed, I have experienced the progress of science and technology from the low technology of the horse and buggy of the early 1900's to the unbelievable global network of interdependent information technology infrastructures, telecommunications and computer processing systems that exist today.

I have witnessed and greatly enjoyed the excitement that was sparked by the ingenious discoveries and developments that have occurred in my lifetime, such as electricity, telephone, radio, automobile, airplane, television, laser beam, computer, atomic fission, rocket propelled travel into outer space, human's first landing on the moon, the first cloning of a mammal and the too numerous to mention achievements in medical, chemical and biological research. Simultaneously, with the passing of the years, I have strived to keep abreast of that progress.

Now, that the twentieth century has come to a close, and the third millenium has begun, Ludmila and I find ourselves caught up in the hub-bub of the computer era. No, we don't have a horse and buggy anymore, but, we do have and still drive our automobile, we have a personal computer and color printer, cell phones, and other modern day electronic and digital conveniences. My life has been a journey through time — from horse and buggy to cyberspace.

Without fear of contradiction, I believe I can safely state that more technological progress was accomplished in the 20th century than in all previous world history. Yet, I envision scientific research and development on the threshold of even greater achievements in the 21st century. However, I hope that the 21st century, new world order of technology (considerably beyond the imagination of so many of us) will be tempered with a moral sense and an attitude of individual professional integrity and corporate ethical conduct.

NO ONE WALKS ALONE

As Ludmila and I walk happily together
down the highway of life,
I reminisce over yesteryear's episodes
and recall life's joys and sorrows.
I, too, bear scars of life's battles.
Days of glory are but fading memories.
Prestige and glamour tempt me no more.
Contentment prevails over foolish yearnings.

When twilight dims and shadows disappear
and in the distance I faintly hear a bugle call,
I'll know that the time is near,
to reach out to Him,
Who has also walked beside me,
As I journeyed down life's highway.
Now, I leave the finale up to Him,
Whatever it is destined to be.

HAIL AND FAREWELL

IN HIS RETIREMENT ADDRESS before congress on April 19, 1951, General Douglas MacArthur said so eloquently, "Old Soldiers never die, they just fade away." For those of you who may wonder, "whatever happened to Old Soldier Colonel Edward A. Trautt," you need only to look toward the horizon of the western sky on the California Pacific Coast, on any day at sunset. There on top of a scenic grass and pine-tree-covered hill, overlooking the Pacific Ocean, visualize old Colonel Ed with his wonderful spouse, companion and sweetheart, Ludmila Perebaskine, in the autumn of their golden years, silhouetted on the horizon, walking hand in hand, waving a fond farewell to all and slowly fading away into the beautifully glowing golden-orange sunset.

So, for our children, grandchildren, great-grandchildren, relatives, and friends, Ludmila and I bid you "Hail and Farewell."

May God bless you with good health,
happiness and good fortune,
as you travel down the winding
and bumpy highway of life,
Cherishing and recording your past,
Vigorously and wisely living your present,
Planning and dreaming your future.

With this farewell, at age 97,
I conclude the writing of this book,
this day of my birth, April 29, 2012.

Made in the USA
Charleston, SC
19 April 2013